OUT
OF
THIN
AIR

OUT OF THIN AIR

by
Betty Rogers Large
and
Tom Crothers

APPLECROSS
PRESS

1989

Design: Ken Shelton

Cover Photography: John Sylvester

Copyediting: Brenda Large

Production: Nancy Murphy, Design and Photo Services.

Wordprocessing: Jan Richardson, Words Unlimited, Kingston, Ont.

Printing: Les Editions Marquis Ltée

ISBN 0-9694205-0-1

Published by
APPLECROSS PRESS
Unit #9, Suite 160
449 University Avenue
Charlottetown, PEI
Canada C1A 8K3

By Mail Postpd., $16.95

Canadian Cataloguing in Publication Data

Large, Betty Rogers, 1913-

    Out of thin air

    Includes bibliographical references.
    ISBN 0-9694205-0-1

1. Rogers, Keith Sinclair. 2. Radio broadcasters -- Prince Edward Island -- Biography. 3. Radio broadcasting -- Prince Edward Island -- History. I. Crothers, Tom. II. Title.

HE8699.C2L37 1989   384.54'09717   C89-098668-1

To the memory of
KEITH SINCLAIR ROGERS

PREFACE

My co-author, Tom Crothers and I, are indebted to the many people who gave interviews and loaned personal memorabilia.

The Canada Council's Explorations Program awarded a grant to Tom in 1983. We gratefully acknowledge this contribution. We also wish to thank Ghislain Malette, Archivist, Public Archives of Canada, the Archivist, Military Museum, Citadel, Halifax, Nova Scotia, Helen MacDonald (Collection, Public Archives of Prince Edward Island) and, Dale McClure of the University of Prince Edward Island Library.

We are grateful to Frank Lewis, Vice President and General Manager of CFCY and MacLean Hunter whose generosity allowed us to have a full color cover.

Deeply appreciated has been the help and encouragement of my daughter, Brenda Large and my Husband, Bob.

Thanks are extended to Ann Bowman, Shirley Partridge, Marjorie Frizzell and Dorothy MacDonald, and the late Loman McAulay for their enthusiasm and help.

Our only regret is that due to lack of space much material had to be omitted.

To the talented people who contributed to the programs, and to CFCY's listeners in five provinces, we trust this book will bring back pleasant memories.

Betty Rogers Large
Charlottetown
Prince Edward Island
1989

CONTENTS

Chapter One

Young Wizards
of the
Airwaves

I remember a time—I couldn't have been more than seven years old about 1920—when we moved to our house on Bayfield Street. Not long ago I went there one evening. The house was shabby. Even the dusk could not hide the peeling paint and broken steps. Some rungs were missing from the verandah railing, giving it an odd gapped-tooth appearance. It had a foolish lopsidedness that even two postage-stamp rectangles of balding lawn on either side of the walk failed to balance. As I stood there in the twilight looking up at the window that once was mine, an unspeakable yearning filled me. Somewhere across the street a child banged a screen door. Suddenly I was back in time, and the memories of childhood came flooding in.

Mother loved to garden. Hardy dahlias lined the front of the house and pink cosmos lined the walk. Window boxes overflowed with bright geraniums. It was a street of children and dogs. All of them, when it came to her garden, were Mother's natural enemy.

The house had seemed so large when I was young. On that now decaying verandah a massive green and white canvas swing, hung by sturdy chains from hooks in the rafters, would hold my sister Marianne who was three, Bill the baby of the family and at least six other children as we played our favourite game of "going somewhere by train". We squabbled noisily over whose turn it was to be conductor and collect the tickets.

Our home seemed the same as almost every other home on the

1

block, except for one thing. Around the back on the second floor was a small verandah of the type housewives used to shake their mops and mats from. Perched precariously on this was a strange contraption in a large black iron frame about five feet high by about three feet across. This was what Dad called the "spark transformer". The door to the back porch was always locked so that we children would not have the unhappy fate of being electrocuted.

At the back of the house Dad had a room called his "wireless shack" and early in the morning and far into the night the clack-clickity-clack-clack of that spark coil transmitter shattered the air, while a brilliant blue spark arced and sputtered from one contact to another. In the dark it could be seen from a mile away. People were frightened of it, and there were ominous murmurings about it being the work of the devil.

On the average of once a week somebody would call the fire station. With bells ringing, children scattering and dogs barking, the fire engine with its leaping firemen would screech to the house. But the only fire there ever was, was in the heated words that would ensue between Dad and the Chief. Then off the engine would go again, careening into the night just as noisily as it had come. After a while the firemen refused to answer any calls to our home. "Just that nut Rogers and his damn blue spark", they'd say. I'm sure if we'd ever had a real fire, the house would have burned to the ground without the benefit of city water or the Charlottetown Volunteer Fire Brigade.

Through all of this my mother remained undismayed. Her worries were concentrated on whatever church she happened to be playing the organ in on Sunday, or on choir practice, funerals or weddings. the idea that the house might be consumed in flames never entered her mind. She diligently banked her small earnings from her work as an organist as survival money. It was her answer to the steady drain on our finances as Dad got more and more into radio.

Our house hummed. It vibrated, it clattered. It was full of excitement, music and strange noises. It abounded with Dad's radio apparatus—we grew up with microphones, control boards, wires, transformers and bits of this and that as naturally as with our toys. At night, after a day of selling insurance, Dad would be building wireless sets for sale. Eventually the living room of that house evolved into what became known as "our Bayfield Street Studio". It was from here that regular radio broadcasts were transmitted between the years 1926-1928. But before he could accomplish this, he had been experimenting for

2

almost nineteen years. It started in 1907 and that year my father, Keith Sinclair Rogers, was just fifteen years old and he had launched himself, using bits of wire, brass screws and round cardboard boxes, and his own adventuresome imagination, into what was to become the age of radio.

He was one of a pioneering band of men around the world, all captivated by "the wireless". The prospect of sending voices and music over the air without wires was then as incredible a dream as our dreams today of travel to faraway planets.

My father's experiments were to carry him, his family and hundreds of colleagues and staff members, into four decades of commercial radio broadcasting in Canada's Maritime Provinces. During those years he would see frail aerials of his boyhood turn into 550-foot transmitting towers sending news, music, entertainment and public affairs into five provinces. More than 300 people would come to work for him and his station—CFCY, The Friendly Voice of the Maritimes.

As a boy, he sent Morse code through the air to a friend down the block. As a man, he and his staff reached hundreds of thousands of people sitting in country kitchens in the dead of winter, or lolling on sunlit summer cottage porches. His work culminated in the construction of a television station; something he wrote into his charter years before it was a reality, calling it "pictures over the air."

There were other broadcasters like my father. In some ways he was typical of the first wave of radio entrepreneurs who founded the industry in Canada. They were experimenters first. Then they saw the business potential, and acted upon it. But they also were keenly interested in public service, in the things they knew radio could do for a community, a province, a country.

In 1907, Keith Rogers was fifteen and he carried a little red book around with him. When I came to write these memories of my father, I found this red book while searching through the family papers. It is an old Army Signal Manual, soiled and worn, thumbed through by two generations of soldiers. You can hold it easily in the palm of your hand. I wondered why he had preserved it so carefully.

Its pages are thick with illustrations of men in uniforms predating the Boer War, demonstrating semiphore flags and signalling lamps. Across its title page my father had written, "C.F.C.Y. Radio Station, Charlottetown, started on the impetus of this 1907 class and this manual." The class referred to were recruits of The No. 12 Signalling Unit, which was the communications section of the old Island regiment,

3

The Prince Edward Island Light Horse—PEI's militia. In those days the signaller's commanding officer was my grandfather, Lt. W.K. Rogers, or "W.K." as he was known around the island.

Grandfather was a self-reliant individualist. During the early days of Canadian railroading he was a telegrapher with the Canadian Pacific and the Great Northern Pacific Railroads. He and Grandma married when he was just eighteen and she just over seventeen. He had to leave for the midwest right after the wedding. Of course her parents were adamant about her not going, but Grandfather had a way with him, and he was able to persuade her father to let her go.

Their first homes were in railroad shacks on the frontiers of Manitoba and Idaho. She spent weeks alone in a cabin with only a young Indian girl for company. What a change the alien and empty prairies were from her home in cosy old Summerside.

W.K. Rogers was interested in cars and foxes. They called him "Good Roads Rogers" because he organized his friends to work on the Island's red clay roads.

I have a striking photograph of Grandfather taken about this time. He is dark-haired with a full mustache, its ends waxed and curling upwards. His firm and determined face is softened by a gentleness in his bright, dark-brown eyes.

"W.K." was vital, energetic and fun-loving. He was always trying new ideas and business ventures; so much so he became a legend in his own lifetime.

In the early days of fox-ranching when PEI was known as the "Silver Fox Capital of the World", he made and lost a million dollars in fox-breeding. He also spearheaded the drive to build the new Prince Edward Island Hospital. He was among those who pioneered the advent of the motor car on the Island, earning himself the nickname "Good Roads Rogers", when he organized gangs of fellow enthusiasts to work to improve the Island's clay roads. The locals said "if there's any sort of pie around, you can bet W.K. has his finger in it."

I write at length about Grandfather because in many ways Dad was so much like him.

Dad inherited his father's tenacity and idealism. But it was an idealism tempered with a strong streak of practicality which always stood him in good stead. Dad was a quiet, reflective child with a head full of bright ideas. Grandmother said when he was a little boy he was as quiet as a little Methodist minister. Grandfather's preoccupations with his many businesses allowed my father enough elbow room to develop his own individuality.

My father's interest in the new "wireless" technology of radio was not shared by my grandfather. It was preposterous to Grandfather that electrical signals could be transmitted from point "A" to point "B" through thin air. After all, as a frontier telegrapher, he had witnessed, first hand, the backbreaking work of stringing thousands of miles of telegraph lines from one end of the country to the other. And now, there was this young scallywag wasting time trying to pull in and transmit through thin air, not only Morse code, but also the human voice and even music. For Grandfather, it was steel rail for trains and steel wire for telegraph.

"Nothing good will ever come from this *wireless* nonsense, Keith. Wireless? Ha! We're simply tangled up in wires. Look at them," he would say.

It was true. The house and family seemed to be tangled up in miles of wire. From the attic came strange whistles and crackles. Up there, my father was completely absorbed for hours—soldering wires and twiddling knobs. When winter came he set up a small kerosene stove. One day it exploded—ignited, no doubt by an arcing spark. Luckily he managed to toss it, flaming, through a dormer window down into the snow, three stories below, where it burned itself out.

Of course, he was ordered to find himself a new and safer place to conduct his "infernal experimenting".

"But I need a quiet place." pleaded Keith.

"A *safe* place." insisted Grandfather. So Dad chose the space behind the bathroom door.

His prudence was offset by the inconvenience to the rest of the family who were forced to line up outside and pound on the door. And no doubt the doorpounding was often accompanied by Grandfather's "No good will ever come from this wireless nonsense, Keith". It was an admonition to be repeated many times during what became known as "Keith's bathroom period".

But a young man driven by a dream tends to be master of all he surveys. Just about everything is seen within the context of that

Keith Rogers experimenting with wireless "behind the bathroom door". 1907.

dream. Stern warnings from irate fathers tend to go unheeded— even to the brink of catastrophe.

Keith was deadly with the brace and bit. His bedroom window-frames were like Swiss cheese. There were even holes drilled in the glass! Countless feet of wire passed through these many holes, travelled up the side of the house and over the roof where they climbed up a pole crudely lashed to the main chimney. From here they stretched out in a four-strand formation high over the yard and street and across to another pole nailed to the gable-end of a barn.

With the exception of his little brother Tom, with whom he shared the bedroom, the rest of the family knew nothing of the aerial. Or if they knew, they certainly paid no attention to it. But the neighbours knew. One stormy day they banged on the door complaining that the wildly swaying, ice-encrusted contraption was about to fall down on their hapless heads.

Grandad hastened to get the ladder. It was gone. The rungs lying in a pile of sawdust were all that was left of it. Looking up, he realized

This aerial on his father's house, 169 Euston Street, was the first of many to be erected by Keith Rogers for wireless, radio and television.

the truth. His good ladder had been quietly spirited away and the sides used to make aerial poles. As Grandfather and the neighbours stood there, wire, poles and even part of the chimney clattered onto the street below. These "poles" fashioned from my Grandfather's good ladder were the first of many communications towers erected by my father— landmarks in his life and in the development of radio on Prince Edward Island.

When he was eventually found, Dad received one of the sternest lectures of his young life. It began of course, with the familiar "Nothing good will ever come from this wireless nonsense, Keith." Only this time it ended louder and sterner with "The insurance business will give you a good living. And you can start learning it by working down at the office after school every day from now on." And donning his coat and hat, Grandfather slammed out of the house, satisfied that he had settled the wireless nonsense for good and headed down to The Charlottetown Club (locally called "The Gentlemen's Club") for his nightly game of billiards. But his warnings, threats, and predictions had fallen on deaf ears.

Like a spider reassembling a wrecked web, Dad scurried back to the apparatus he had been working on as soon as his father was off the front porch.

He needed coils. So he raided his mother's pantry for round oatmeal boxes because they made excellent coils if you wound copper wire tightly around them. The contents were dumped unceremoniously into whatever dish was handy. He already had his ground, the lead pipe in the bathroom. But he needed brass screws.

No doubt Grandfather was at the club convinced that Keith was at home contrite and reflecting on his follies. Not a bit of it. Instead, he was methodically removing every large nut and screw from his parents' large brass bed. He intended, of course, to put them all back before Grandfather returned; so he very carefuly left the bed standing— precariously, in limbo.

Now, as it happened, billiards like the rest of the day had not gone too well for Grandfather and to Keith's horror he heard the front door bang followed by his father's heavy footsteps coming up the stairs. A tired man threw himself on the bed. The bed collapsed, shaking the house and knocking the plaster off the ceiling below and filling his mother's cherished carpet with lime. A litany of curses, hitherto unheard of in that sedate home, arose from the debris along with cries of anguish

8

calling for the Sloan's Liniment. By the time he had put the bed together, my father had heard enough to convince him, never again, to disturb the sanctity of that brass bed for wireless parts.

One would think this episode would have finished Dad's experimenting once and for all, but fortunately—to my grandparents' credit—their sense of humour and tolerance helped them outride the storm and he was allowed to continue. Dad of course, did his "penance" in the office of the family insurance business, a business which was to be both a blessing and a nemesis. Just as it sustained "W.K." through rough times in the fox business, it was to sustain Dad through rough times in the radio business.

Shortly after the bed episode the young wireless enthusiast enjoyed a victory. He convinced Grandfather there might be something to "this wireless nonsense" after all.

One day Dad managed to pick up some signals on his set. "W.K." listened in, and through the crackling distortions he recognized Morse code! The old telegrapher must have been excited and proud. No steel wire—just a contraption using a few strands of light aerial wire picking up signals. Keith's role as an experimenter was given more respect, and his father's intolerance changed to encouragement. Grandma Rogers though, was still somewhat distraught over the disruption in her home as Dad acquired more coils, condensers, capacitors and wire. His little brother Tom was forced to move to another bedroom.

My mother told me she met my father while they were both attending the vice-principal's class in high school. "I fell head-over-heels in love with him, but he was head-over-heels in love with wireless." Mother was able to disentangle him enough, however, to make him notice her, and eventually they became sweethearts.

When she made her first visit to the Rogers home she was greeted with enthusiasm by my grandmother who thought Mother could take Dad's mind off his wireless "obsession". Grandma warned her, "You've no idea what you're getting yourself into. Since he started this experimenting business nothing's safe. Last week he took my sewing machine apart trying to get it to wind up those coil things."

But mother was not discouraged. He fitted up her room at home with a miniature sending-receiving set, and soon Morse code messages were flashing back and forth from the Rogers' to the Smiths'.

"Hello F.S. (Flora Smith)...K calling. I love you. Do you still love me?"

9

Flora Smith in 1911

*Flora and Keith at Brackley Beach on a picnic with
another couple.*

But Mother said he was reassured rather slowly because she could never get her speed up. After a courtship of six years, they married at age twenty-one, on May 7, 1913.

During the decade prior to World War I, the army was keenly interested in wireless telegraphy as radio was known then. Although basic training for signallers was still based mainly on the use of flags and lamps, the armed forces encouraged experimentation with wireless. Indeed, the first government licences issued to wireless communicators were to militia units. One of the earliest in Canada—XAR—was issued in 1909, to my father, at the Charlottetown Armoury.

Also during these years, the number of enthusiasts for the new technology was growing. In Charlottetown they tended to gravitate toward the No. 12 Signalling Unit. Wireless was in. The Canadian Coastguard was using it to great advantage. In the winter of 1909, Dad got a job for seven months as wireless operator aboard the ice-breaker *Minto* relieving the regular operator who was taking time off because his wife was having a baby.

Two years later, Grandfather retired as commanding officer of the No. 12 Signalling Unit and Dad, now Lt. K.S. Rogers, replaced him.

Around father gathered a group of devotees who, as well as learning from him in the militia, also took a course from him at the Y.M.C.A.

Today when we hear a term like "militiaman" an image of a grown man, armed to the teeth, comes to mind. But the militiamen of the No. 12 Signals were young boys. One of them, Major General "Bunny" Weeks, CB, CBE, MC, MM, CD, Rtd., recalled that his mother, because it was raining, wouldn't let him go on a dress parade to be inspected by Sir Ian Hamilton, unless he wore his rubber boots.

In the summer of 1911, Father and his squad built the first successful portable military wireless set in Canada at Petawawa military camp near Ottawa. Today we think of mobile sets as being compact. But this early "portable" wireless pack-set required two horses to drag it onto the field and four men to carry it when horse-power wasn't available.

It must be difficult for people born into the high technology era of today to appreciate the excitement felt by the radio pioneers of those days. In old sepia photographs of them posing self-consciously beside antique and cumbersome equipment, they look quaint and unsophisticated. Nothing could be further from the truth.

In their day, they were the sophisticates. They were the astronauts of the airwaves. They lived in a time when people who heard voices

11

of others who were not there, were considered madmen, visionaries, or spiritualists. Today we take the terminology of communications coined by them for granted. The Greek words *Telos* meaning "from afar" and *Phone*, meaning "voice" give us magical words like *telephone*. Wireless Telephone to them meant "voices coming from afar without wire." Remember, today's "high tech" is built upon yesterday's high tech.

Marconi portable field wireless. The Citadel, Halifax, N.S., 1914.

Heliograph signalling. Citadel, Halifax 1915.

Signalling by flags. First World War.

Wireless Telegraphy—"writing from afar," in this early decade of the twentieth century, was considered a tremendous advance over the telegraph wires of my grandfather's day. It also was regarded as being in advance of the telephone, which even today still requires cable, or wire.

Wireless telegraphy is the parent of modern radio communications. In those days the dream was to carry the **human voice** without wires. Just as the telegraph of Morse gave way to the telephone of Alexander Graham Bell, wireless telegraphy was to give way to wireless telephony, or radio. As early as 1906 the Canadian inventor Reginald Fessenden successfully transmitted the human voice and music on the mysterious radio waves.

A few years back I was fortunate to talk to Group Captain Ronnie Stewart—now deceased—at his home in Ottawa when he was Private Secretary to the then Governor General, Lord Tweedsmuir. As a boy Captain Stewart had been one of Dad's group of signallers. Without hesitation he reached back seventy odd years into the past and recalled names, details, and incidents as clearly as if they happened yesterday:

> *In the old days, Ernest Auld, Keith Rogers and Harold Pickard were interested in wireless and "Bunny" Weeks and I became interested as well. Keith was the mainspring and he was far advanced in the theories of wireless.*

I wish I could share with you the excitement and enthusiasm that came alive in Group Captain Stewart as he recounted the first time he heard the human voice without wires in 1911! The best I can do is to quote his own words:

> *I'll give you this as a never-to-be-forgotten experience of mine. One day in 1911, on an April Saturday morning. The fog was heavy—it had been raining and drizzling all night, and dampness was everywhere, and I was adjusting my wireless set, when to my amazement and astonishment, I heard a neighbour ordering her groceries! Now that was the spoken word, to me,— without wires! I doubt if there are many people, living today, who have had that experience so far back.*

13

Of course what Group Captain Stewart heard was not a voice transmitted through radio. Instead, it was due to induction caused by the damp weather. But the fact he heard it *verified* how it was possible for the human voice to travel without wires!

Another exciting event, in 1912, was experienced by a member of that group, Ernest Auld. Ernie received, directly by wireless, much of the news about the Titanic's sinking long before many of the local newspapers.

Many of the fourteen or fifteen boys who gathered around my father during this period went to war when the conflict broke out in 1914. I have a photograph of several of them—those who were especially close—being driven to their embarkment by my father. Dad, too, was called, and shortly after he said farewell to the boys in his squad he moved with his young family to Halifax taking up duty there as the Fortress Signal's Officer, at the Citadel.

Credit PAPEI

Capt. Keith S. Rogers, driving. Others are: Cpl Ernest G. Weeks, Signalman George W. Gardner, Vernon H. MacLeod, Heber R. Large, Harry W. Whitlock, H. Ronald Stewart.

Chapter Two

Sounds
from
Faraway Schenectady

When Dad was posted to Halifax in 1914, I was barely a year old. My sister Marianne was born there in October 1917, about six weeks before the tragic Halifax explosion. To help with the house Dad hired a maid, a girl named Sylvia Publicover who came from a place with the strange old name of Ecum Secum. We had an apartment within walking distance of the Citadel on Williams Street, which meant Dad could live at home when he was not on duty.

At that time the Citadel was a military intelligence center so it is difficult to ascertain precisely what Dad's duties were there. I know from his papers that he continued his research and experimentation in wireless. From a receiving apparatus of his own construction, he was able to pull in, directly from Berlin and Paris, official communiques of the German and French general staffs. These were logged daily, and the information was forwarded to Ottawa. So it seems, through the years 1915-17, he was involved in some sort of wireless surveillance— probably one of the earliest forms of electronic surveillance in the history of warfare.

His routine duty at the Citadel was the maintainance of communications by visual telegraph—lamps and flags—and wireless telegraph with the various units comprising the fortress. During this period he was also seconded to the Royal School of Infantry and the Royal School of Artillery to train wireless operators. At age 23, he was promoted to Captain and placed in charge of all communications including the military telephone system. Each year he applied for overseas service, but his applications were turned down—much I'm sure to my Mother's relief—on the grounds of necessity for his service in Canada.

I was too young to have any conscious memories of Halifax; but the story of what happened when it was devastated by the explosion caused by the collision of two munition ships, the *Imo* and the *Mont Blanc*, has been told so often, it seems as if I actually do remember it—so I'll tell it that way.

It started just like any ordinary day. We were sitting around the breakfast table. Mother always said that if Dad had not had such quick reflexes, all of us, except baby Marianne, would have been killed. We had large dining-room windows, and as we looked out, we could see the man next door up on a ladder fixing his house. Suddenly, there was an awesome feeling of danger as an ominous swishing noise filled the air.

"Under the table!" my father roared, grabbing me and throwing me to the floor. Sylvia, the maid, flung herself across Marianne's bassinet. As we huddled there pressed to the floor a shower of glass flew over us, embedding itself in the far wall. Shards of it had to be taken out of poor Sylvia's back. I still carry the scar where it cut my knee. The man next door was blown off his ladder, his body found over in the next street.

Dad reported immediately to the Citadel, but before he went he took us to the Commons where the military was erecting a sort of tent city to house the thousands of fleeing homeless. We spent the night there in the open because there was fear of a second explosion. Outside, it was bitter cold; and to add to the misery, there was a heavy snowfall throughout the night which turned into a blizzard the next day.

Death, fear, and pain were everywhere as thousands of victims lay in long rows at the hospitals and receiving stations waiting their turn to be attended or pronounced dead. Dad said people reacted quickly and courageously. Military and naval units organized search and rescue parties. Firemen fought desperately to bring raging fires under control. Doctors and nurses were operating as soon as schools, halls, churches and private homes could be set up as temporary hospitals. Special trains were arranged to bring help from the United States and the rest of Canada.

Immediately the news of the explosion reached the Island, Grandfather "W.K.", who was chairman of the PEI Hospital Board, organized a team of doctors and nurses and a cavalcade of cars to go to Halifax. All the Island roads were blocked with snow. Undeterred, they drove the cars along the railroad tracks. When he arrived at the stricken city, Grandfather went straight to our home, stuck his head in at the door and called out, "Is everyone alive and well?" Satisfied we were, he left at once for the Red Cross Headquarters.

Those people with friends or relatives elsewhere who could take them in were evacuated from the city. Mother, Marianne and I were sent home along with many others on the Borden train. When we landed at the station in Charlottetown, men walked ahead of us on the platform calling to the crowds, "Make way for the Halifax refugees!" We remained on the Island for the duration of the war.

The train from the ferry at Borden was fondly called "The Borden Train." Circa 1910.

Dad was released from active service on February 1, 1919. He had gained a great deal of experience and knowledge during his five years in the army, and the dream of radio and its potential was stronger than ever in him.

Philosophically, Dad saw radio as a means of closing gaps in people's lives. Through the airwaves each part of the world could give to the

17

other the best it had to offer—a world that was still reeling from the shock and horror of the Great War—a war that was supposed to end all war. The climate of the early twenties was right for builders and dreamers.

In later life Dad would roll off his tongue a whole litany of heroes, all of them early inventors in radio: Edison, Fressenden, Tesla, Steinmetz, Marconi, Flemming, Kettering and a host of other lesser known scientist- inventors. "All of their wonderful inventions culminated in the invention of the three element radiotron, or audiotron developed by Dr. Lee Deforest." he said. It was this, the audiotron, a vacuum tube containing three elements which allowed man to control radio waves. "This modern Alladin's Lamp is destined to change, in one way or another, the life of every human being on this planet," Dad said.

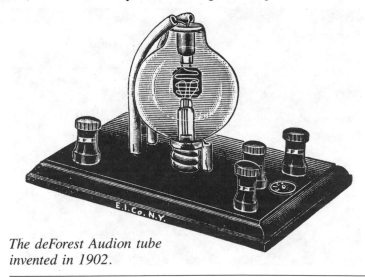

*The deForest Audion tube
invented in 1902.*

He was right. It made possible the development of radar, television, the electron microscope and just about every modern sophisticated piece of electronic wonder commonplace today.

But the reality of all these wonderful inventions was twenty to thirty years away. In the meantime, the need to earn a living kept him selling insurance. Our family was expanding; my brother Bill was soon to be born. It would be wrong for me to say the insurance business was a drudge, because he enjoyed it. It gave him a chance to get around the

18

Island and talk to people—not to mention the chance it gave him to get in a little trout fishing. Sometimes during the summer we would go with him, tenting on the grounds of a country school while he made his calls. Yet radio was still a part of his life. Captivated as he was, he kept experimenting and planning until the time was right to get into it more deeply.

I suppose it was inevitable for father and son to have differences of opinion as to how things should be done—especially when both were so strong-minded. So Dad decided to go into the insurance business for himself. "W.K." agreed, but urged him not to leave the company but to work independently within it. So instead of moving out of the office, Grandfather simply set Dad up with a section of his own, and they remained good friends.

About this time, Dad was made the provincial representative of Canada Life and did so well he was made a member of the "Million Dollar Club". Shortly after, he was promoted to provincial manager and the commissions he earned helped carry the family through some very lean times to come.

But the lure of wireless was still too strong for him to shake it entirely, and in 1920-21, he taught a class in electricity and wireless communications to eighteen or twenty young men at the Provincial Technical School. The Technical School was a classroom in the Rena MacLean Memorial Hospital, which at that time was being used for the convalescence of wounded veterans. Dad organized a radio club for

After the First World War, Government House became the Rena MacLean Convalescent hospital.

19

those men who were able and interested. It was here on March 11, 1921 that he and his class heard the first radio concert ever to be received on Prince Edward Island.

They had been picking up regular ship-to-shore messages in Morse code on the wireless receiver he had built. But on that particular March evening they suddenly heard what sounded like music and speech. It was fading badly, but once in a while it became crystal clear. Imagine the excitement and intensity in that classroom now transformed into a Prospero's cave as each anxiously took his turn with the head-set to hear those miraculous sounds coming through.

Quite by chance they had tuned in students at Union Technical College in Schenectady, New York, who were conducting transmitting experiments with a gramaphone and a wheezy player-piano. It was indeed an exciting breakthrough. Dad lost no time getting in touch with Union Tech to offer congratulations and to exchange technical information. Of course the boys in Schenectady were delighted to hear they had been received in Canada, and they agreed to make a special broadcast for Prince Edward Island the following week.

Meanwhile at home, Dad busied himself. This was an event not to be missed. He made arrangements not only for the press to attend, but the Premier, most of the Cabinet, the Mayor of Charlottetown, several judges and prominent businessmen. But how could so many—there were thirty-seven in all—listen in on one headphone set? He solved it by improvising a loudspeaker attached to an earpiece from the headset to a large brass phonograph horn—the kind the famous fox terrier listened to his master's voice through.

When the big night arrived the honoured guests were seated in the front row close to the loudspeaker. The crowded classroom was filled with cigar-smoke and expectation. What followed was truly a unique experience for all of them. Conditions were unreliable and static was bad, but Dad twiddled the tuning knob persistently. He was using the same receiver he had built at the Citadel, and after all, if he had been able to tune in Paris and Berlin, surely he could get Schenectady, New York again.

Yet nothing but hisses and an undulating whistle were heard through the horn. The boys in the class sat with their fingers crossed sharing an intensity of the kind you see shared by fans when they hope their favourite team will score the winning goal. The guests looked at each other as the horn continued to emit its whistles and crackles. Just as

20

cynicism was setting in the miracle happened. From the loud speaker came a wavering, tinny voice saying:

This is Union Technical College in Schenectady, calling. Tonight we send cordial greetings to our friends in Charlottetown, Prince Edward Island, Canada, and hope you are receiving our transmission.

Then followed some tinkling piano music which faded in and out for a time and finally disappeared altogether.

Scepticism turned to enthusiam. In those days of still mainly horse and buggy travel the physical distance between Schenectady and Charlottetown was fairly great. Yet here was living proof that the great physical distances could be transcended by the twiddle of a knob. I wonder if any of those politicians as they sat there listening calculated in their minds the powerful future use of radio. I know my father did.

Chapter Three

Bringing in
the
Dempsey Fight

B y 1922 the transmission of voice and music was happening all over the world. From the larger centers in the United States, the Radio Corporation of America was broadcasting music and lectures by famous scientists, and in the British Isles and continental Europe similar things were happening. Today, there are thousands of stations broadcasting all around the globe twenty-four hours a day. But in the early twenties there were only a few stations in the world broadcasting for just a few hours each day. The technology, however, was developing with the speed of a brush fire, and each day the number of broadcasters increased.

The earliest type of receiver was the crystal set which consisted of a dry cell battery, a coil, a small crystal of graphite, and a cat's whisker—which was a fine piece of copper wire soldered to a small pivoting arm. The operator donned a pair of earphones and then patiently and gently scratched the surface of the crystal until he was able, if he was lucky, to pick up some primitive broadcaster.

The crystal set soon gave way to the more sophisticated tube-type receivers. These too, were made by people like Dad. The revenue from them in the beginning helped pay for the very expensive parts needed for experiments.

In the spring of 1921, my father had the only experimental radio license in the province—the 10-watt 9AK using batteries for all power. In the fall of 1921 under this license he began broadcasting both announcements and phonograph programs. The broadcasting was

Courtesy of Edna Burke Rodd

Early receiver 1925 built by Keith Rogers
for Walter Burke.

sporadic as he was constantly building and re-building equipment.

The fall of the year 1922 stands out vividly in my mind. I was nine years old and that was the year Dad broadcast music to his booth at the Provincial Exhibition. We had red, white and blue cheesecloth bunting to hang, flags to tack up, with red maple leaves and long strands of golden wheat. The huge old Victorian-type building sported fall colors from one end of the building to the other, and there was much noise and excitement as this agricultural fair attracted all the farm families on the Island for the judging of the harvest. Many had never heard a radio before and very few had actually seen a receiving set. I remember being surprised that music broadcast from our house, which to me seemed miles and miles away, could be heard so clearly at the exhibition grounds.

There were only four other experimental stations in the Maritimes

23

PAPEI

Provincial Exhibition Building. Destroyed by
fire, April 25, 1945.

at that time: Acadia University, Wolfville with 9AT; F.P. Vaughn, Saint
John 9BI; F. G. O'Brien 9BL at the Nova Scotia Technical College,
Halifax and the Marconi Wireless Telegraph Co. in Newcastle with 9BN.
They were all experimenting with what was called *radiophone.*

During this time Dad and his friend and co-experimentalist Walter
Hyndman, who was some ten years younger than Dad, built and rebuilt
several transmitters. The dream had always been to build a transmitter
that would send **voice** as well as receive it. By 1921 the technology to
do this was available, but the cost to hobbyists of limited means was
prohibitive. And there were certain types of tubes that were virtually
impossible to get—especially on PEI.

One summer an American warship equipped with the most up-to-
date radio technology visited Charlottetown. Walter Hyndman
befriended the chief wireless officer who gave him a present of radio
tubes that could not be bought locally. Walter built a small transmitter
for **voice** and code.

Walter, although only in his teens, was well-versed in wireless telegraphy and was the chief operator and instructor at the Navy League.
The Evening Patriot called him "a wizard at the wireless." He had built
his five-watt transmitter following instructions in an article he had read
in Radio News, a magazine for wireless enthusiasts. On April 22, 1921

24

the Patriot reported:

CHARLOTTETOWN BOY ON ROAD TO ENGINEERING FAME

Radio News, a magazine published in New York in the interests of Experimental Wireless Telegraphy, has in its April number a very well written article by Walter Hyndman, the seventeen year old son of Mr. W.E. Hyndman of the Department of Public Works of this city.

He has taken an article published in the November issue of the same magazine and by considerable thought and work, developed this article into working plans from which anyone interested may construct a similar piece of apparatus. The power of imagination which enabled him to place all the various switches and controls in the most convenient position for the operator are especially to be praised.

The 1922 list at the Public Archives in Ottawa prints the names of 14 enthusiastic amateur station operators in PEI. As well as Walter Hyndman, there was G.G. Houston, Charlottetown,—Dr. "Gil" Houston whose hobby for a lifetime was "ham" radio. In Summerside, there was Harold Gaudet, and Messrs Whitney, Mackie, MacKay and Pritchard. And there were many others including Walter Burke of Charlottetown.

Walter Burke was one of the newer kind of enthusiasts, those with a limited technical knowledge who not only read everything they could get their hands on about radio but they spent all their spare time on it. Dad built Walter Burke his first radio receiver in the winter of 1921. Walter Burke was about twenty years older than my father and some thirty years older than Walter Hyndman, but they were were all working for the same goal—to develop this new form of communication.

By 1922, Station KDKA Pittsburg, one of the earliest broadcasting stations in North American, could be heard in Charlottetown. Mr. Burke, a devout Methodist, heard a religious service and was immediately inspired with the idea of broadcasting services from his own church, the First Methodist, in Charlottetown.

*F. Walter Hyndman, a
pioneer in amateur wireless
and radio.*

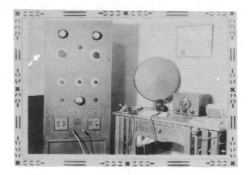

*VEIBZ, Walter Hyndman's
amateur wireless station
(100 Watts). About 1930.*

Courtesy of Edna Burke Rodd

*Walter E. Burke, Charlottetown.Early
pioneer broadcaster.*

At this time Dad was operating several transmitters under the call
letters 9AK. It was, strictly speaking, illegal. But licencing procedures
had not been formalized, and at times the question of illegal or legal
operation was moot.

For example, equipment was built and rebuilt and parts
interchanged—it was difficult to tell where an original set started and
a new one began. At this point experimentalists like Dad, Walter Burke,
and Walter Hyndman were all good friends who co-operated and
exchanged knowledge and ideas freely with each other. The experimenters then, were the future's broadcasters. What was going on in
Charlottetown was typical of what was going on in the rest of the
country. In a few years when their amateur stations were changed to

professional, the situation changed. Old co-operating and sharing friends became professional competitors.

Walter Hyndman was broadcasting over his newly-made transmitter one evening, and Walter Burke picked him up on his receiver. He promptly paid the younger Walter a visit and persuaded him to sell the transmitter. A few months later it was licenced under the call letters 1CK. At first he used Morse code only, but in the summer of 1922 it became a small broadcasting station. This was about nine months after my father commenced broadcasting.

Until this time the transmission of the human voice, without wires, had been one-way only. But with what was called the new continuous wave method of radio, Dad impressed his voice on his 9AK transmitter and spoke to Walter Hyndman who was operating another transmitter a few blocks away in the Navy League building in Charlottetown. Walter spoke back; and so, by using the same method of modulation, the human voice was carried **two-way** on radio waves originating in Charlottetown.

The number of hobby-experimentalists in wireless-telegraph and radio-telephone was increasing greatly. I suppose a parallel could be drawn with the number of computer hobbyists there are today as that technology develops. Clubs and leagues sprang up in an attempt to control, standardize, and share information. The most influential of these by far in North America was the Amateur Radio Relay League, in Hartford, Connecticut. Dad organized the Maritime provinces and was appointed their first divisional inspector, an appointment he held until 1923.

It is estimated by 1922 there were fifty or more receivers on the Island. By the following year, the figure doubled. Receivers ranged from the very primitive crystal sets to the more advanced "howlers"—so called because they let out an unmerciful scream if not tuned properly. A few years later, Dad went on a personal quest to collect as many of these as he could and dump them. That was when the very sophisticated two to five tube-sets had come on the market.

Reception on the Island was doubtful at all times, especially during the daylight hours. Indeed reception was so critical, daytime broadcasts were practically non-existent as far as Islanders were concerned. Nevertheless, people were catching the radio bug and more and more of them were equipping their homes with receivers. The rush for sets was on. The increasing demand provided the beginnings of a small business which later grew to be the Island Radio Broadcasting Co. Ltd.

In the meantime people who could afford their Radio Telephone Concert Receivers, as they called them, were ordering them. As the demand for sets grew so did the demand that pushed Dad into the business of selling radios in a more formal way. Coupled with this was his concern over the daytime broadcasting silences when it was difficult to tune in the larger stations broadcasting from the U.S. and mainland Canada. He got a brainwave. Why not do some broadcasting during these silent periods as well as sell sets?

Now one of the oldest retail businesses in Charlottetown was the Rogers Hardware Company. Established in 1852, it occupied a site on what is now called Confederation Square. The Rogers family, who are distantly related to mine, still run a smaller store in the city. The old store itself had undergone little apparent re-modelling. Its high embossed ceilings, plank floors and long wooden counters exuded an atmosphere of conservatism and sedate courtesy. The large old-fashioned windows look out defiantly at the ultra modern Confederation Center of the Arts across the street. It was from the Rogers Hardware Company that Dad did some of his first broadcasting in the early twenties.

Photo by Wong

Rogers Hardware an historic landmark.

I found the letterhead my father used. It proclaims:

KEITH S. ROGERS
Dealer in Experimental Radio Apparatus
Station, Canadian 9AK

Written below the letterhead is an order signed by Ivan J. Reddin to purchase a Radio Telephone Concert Receiver. The building and complete installation came to $310.00—a large sum at that time.

By 1922 Rogers Hardware was already 70 odd years old and was a hardware store in the real sense of the word—dealing in the no-nonsense business of selling anvils, tools, steel chain, fencing and horse harness. It must, therefore, have been with a sense of misgiving that the elder Mr. Rogers agreed to enter into something as new-fangled as the radio business.

Keep in mind that young men like Dad, as are all young men in every age who are ahead of their time, were generally regarded as being a bit odd. For example, Walter Hyndman recalled overhearing a woman say as he walked past her, "There's that young fellow who says he hears angel's voices in the air." However, Mr. Rogers agreed to open a radio department in the hardware store on a sharing arrangement with Dad.

Under the baleful eye of the senior hardware man, an appropriate display was set up. In the store window by a small five watt transmitter—the one originally built by Walter Hyndman—a microphone, and a wind-up gramaphone were installed. And to catch the attention of passers-by, he put up a loudspeaker-horn over the outside door. Another speaker was mounted on a shelf above the new Radio Department.

These storefront broadcasts, primitive as they were, were picked up and well-received in Wood Islands, Murray Harbour, Summerside, and even as far away as Pictou and New Glasgow, Nova Scotia. He broadcast daily, excepting Sunday, for about an hour at noon and later for a spell in the afternoon. He later sold radios that were installed by Angus MacMasters and two helpers, young Bill Hunt and Reg Jenkins. If there was something of special interest, he would do his best to receive and broadcast it—like the famous Dempsey vs. Firpos fight. Apparently as the word got around, Queen Street was lined with horses and wagons and the boardwalk outside Rogers Hardware was crowded with men.

Rogers Hardware circa 1900. Minstrel
parade foreground.

We take radio so much for granted today it is difficult to imagine the impact it made on those who were hearing it for the first time. Mrs. Ellie Grant, a ninety-four year old resident of James River, Antigonish County, Nova Scotia remembers very clearly what broadcasting was like fifty years ago:

The first time I ever heard radio was on a receiver owned by Jack MacGregor, who was the wireless operator at the James River Railway Station. My father loved the boxing. He was getting on and he heard that Jack Dempsey, his great idol, was boxing Firpos and he also heard that they were going to try to broadcast it. So I went down with him to the Railway Station and sure enough, the fight was on, and it was coming through Charlottetown. That was the first time, now, I ever heard radio and my father too. Well you can imagine how excited he was. Up to that time the only contact he ever had with Jack Dempsey was reading about him in the newspapers.

31

A strange thing I remember about radio was that a man who lived near us would always get into his good clothes and sit in front of his radio. He was not the only one to do this, all kinds of people would do this. It was a very special thing you see, and they wanted to be dressed correctly for it.

Before we got our own radio we'd go to other homes to listen. And we would sit there and stare at the radio, and we'd continue listening even though the crashes of the static would wipe out the broadcasting entirely.

One time we were visiting the static was very bad; the lady of the house got up to make a lunch, and we were all ready to take the earphones off, but "No" she said, "leave them on." and we sat there eating lunch and listening to static. It became a very social thing, visiting and listening to radio. The marvel *of it...we just couldn't understand how it worked at all.*

Weekdays, while Dad was broadcasting from the hardware store, his friend Walter Burke was broadcasting an hour of sacred music and readings every Sunday afternoon from his living room on Upper Hillsboro Street. Toombs Music Store in Charlottetown loaned both Dad and Mr. Burke phonograph records in exchange for advertising.

In the meantime, Walter Burke, after a few months of successful Sunday broadcasting over his tiny 1CK "amateur radio telephone", was still more determined than ever to broadcast from his church. He called on Walter Hyndman to see if he could build him a bigger transmitter, a professional-like one, something around twenty watts.

"How much will it cost me?" he asked Hyndman.

"Plenty, I'm afraid", Walter Hyndman replied.

When the cost was estimated, it was several hundred dollars. Walter Burke was not a wealthy man. He worked for the old Charlottetown wholesaler, Carter and Company, in their seed department. But he was dedicated to the idea of broadcasting church services. He was a great Methodist and had been listening to religious services from KDKA. It now became his life's ambition and he was ready to start raising money. Mrs. Burke, also an avid churchgoer, agreed to go along, and Walter Hyndman was given the go-ahead to build a twenty watt station for him.

The transmitter was an ambitious project. It had a normal daylight range of 25 miles, and a seventy foot wire cage aerial stretched between two wooden poles fifty feet high. The local wireless enthusiasts helped to set up the new station at Walter Burke's residence on Upper Hillsborough street. When everything was in working order, the only thing needed was a licence.

To operate such a station, there were two classes of licences: a commercial licence, and an amateur broadcasting club licence. To get the commercial one, the applicant had to have a bona fide business. Walter Burke, who did not own a business, did not qualify for a commercial licence. Dad visited several friends and a club was formed. Its formation was reported in the Charlottetown Guardian:

Last evening a radio club, the Charlottetown Radio Association, was formed in town. President, Judge Arsenault, Vice-president, Keith Rogers, Secretary Treasurer, C.K.R. Steeves. Members at large are J.A.S. Bayer, Walter S. Grant, Walter O. Hyndman, Walter E. Burke, and Vivian Smallwood.

The Charlottetown Radio Association provided the legal basis for getting an operating licence in much the same way as clubs are formed to qualify for a liquor licence. The club made its application, and on July 31st, 1923, a licence was granted under the call letters of 10AS. The installation and subsequent licencing of 10AS was a source of jubilation and pride to Dad, Walter Hyndman, Walter Burke and the members of the club. Walter Hyndman noted in his diary, "As of this day, 10AS is under club licence."

The Burke household was a hive of activity. Broadcasting was taking hold on the Island. Dad was making his daily broadcasting from Rogers Hardware, and Walter Burke extended his sacred hour from Sunday to Wednesday evenings as well. All the enthusiasts were planning, adjusting and rebuilding. Walter Hyndman, though, was withdrawing from wireless to devote more time to the family insurance business.

In the meantime they planned the first church service broadcast for Sunday morning, January 25, 1925. All the previous week they set up, tested and re-tested equipment in the church. Mr. Ryan, the minister, was particularly anxious for the broadcast to work. His wife, a chronic invalid, had not heard him preach for several years.

When Sunday finally came, it was snowy and cold, but the church was packed. All over the Island, those who owned radios turned them on. Because the broadcasters were known personally, and the program was of great local significance, the excitement was intense. I wonder if many people dressed in their Sunday best to listen.

From the moment the choir sang the Doxology to the closing hymn, the program went off without a hitch. It was the second church broadcast in Canada, and the first east of Winnipeg. The first actual Canadian church broadcast originated from Winnipeg a few months earlier.

The response was overwhelming. Mail came from all over the Island and from the mainland as well. Remarks made by Miss Marion Ryan, the daughter of Rev. Ryan, who preached the sermon, capture some of the feeling generated by that broadcast:

...mail began to pour in...from places in P.E.I., N.B., N.S. and the New England states. These letters were from shut-ins and people who, for various reasons were not able to attend church. All spoke of the clarity of reception and of the happiness and blessing it was to be able to share in a service of worship... nowhere did it mean as much as it did in our home. Mother was confined to bed in the parsonage for almost three years. The women of the congregation presented her with a radio—the kind one listened to through earphones...she was able to hear my father preach for the first time in many years...I will never forget her joy...in being able to share in the music and the messages from the church so near at hand—yet so inaccessible to her.

The future of church broadcasting on the Island assured, the demand for radios increased. As people clamoured for sets, the demand for batteries and parts grew. So did the number of broadcasts. Increasingly, radio was becoming a part of life.

A number of manufacturing concerns were buying up patents and getting into the business of mass producing radios. One of these, the DeForest-Crossley Corporation, approached Dad to carry its line, as did other manufacturers. His new letterhead shows how much he had expanded within a year. It sports a picture of a deluxe Deforest-Crossley radio, flanked on either side by an impressive list of radio equipment manufacturers being handled by The Island Radio Company. The banner now was in gothic script.

Shortly after Dad took on the Deforest-Crossley dealership, a competitor appeared on the scene. The Marconi Corporation appointed James A. Gesner as its dealer. Jim Gesner had a welding and vulcanizing business. In another few years he was to play a leading role as Dad's competitor in the broadcasting business as well.

Chapter Four

CFCY
Goes
On The Air

After the success of the first and subsequent church broadcasts, Dad tried to persuade Walter Burke to go commercial. But Walter was reluctant to expand. He was not a businessman. He had put enough into 10AS, and it was doing what he wanted it to do.

Dad and Mr. Burke, since that first church broadcast, were working almost as partners. Dad supplied tube replacement and maintenance for 10AS, and continuous technical help in setting up for the church broadcasts. In return, he received direct advertising for his retail radio store, The Island Radio. In 1925, the partnership became a reality. During the winter months of 1924 my father and Walter Burke had worked long hours together re-building the transmitter in order that it could be licenced for fifty watts power. This licence was granted to them in 1925. My father wrote the letters to the Department of Marine and had the frequency changed to 960 on the dial. This was a greater advantage to the station although it took some persuasion for the Department to make the change.

Walter Burke was persuaded to expand, for on June 8, 1925, Dad wrote to Ottawa requesting a commercial licence under the call letters CPEI—meaning Charlottetown, Prince Edward Island.

He was advised that the call letters CPEI were not available, "but if he would be good enough to fill out the enclosed application form and enclose a cheque for $50.00 his application would be given serious consideration." He was also advised that if his application were successful, he would have to share the same frequency with Canadian National

Railways, Moncton, and with another station in Mont Joli, Quebec.

The application was filled and duly sent off with the fee enclosed. In an enclosed letter he accused Ottawa of discriminating against the Maritimes by its allocation of only one wavelength for such a large region, while Toronto and Montreal had several times that allocated to each of them. This initiated a flurry of memoranda up and down the bureaucratic ladder, causing a delay in the granting of the licence. Ten days passed and there was still no letter or word on his application. Dad was impatient and eager. He had sent off his application and $50.00—a lot of money—why wasn't there a reply? Unable to stand the suspense any longer, he fired off a cable. Two days later, on August 10, 1925, he received the following reply:

LICENCE MAILED TODAY STOP
YOU WILL SHARE THREE HUNDRED
METERS WITH MONCTON FOR TIME BEING
STOP CALL SIGN CFCY STOP REPEAT
CFCY

But when the licence, #42—the first commercial licence issued to Prince Edward Island, and the first commercial licence in Eastern Canada—arrived in the mail, an accompanying letter advised that Moncton had been assigned a new wavelength. CFCY didn't have to share its frequency.

Even though they were now partners in the first commercial station on PEI, Walter Burke and Dad each had his own personal broadcasting dream. Mr. Burke's was to broadcast local church services. The Burke family had sacrificed a great deal to purchase 10AS and to have it installed to do just this. Dad's dream was more secular. He envisioned a powerful station—as powerful as some of the future Toronto or American stations. And why not, he reasoned. Didn't the air belong to everybody?

While researching the period 1925-1928 at the National Archives in Ottawa, I was amazed at the hefty amount of correspondence between CFCY and Ottawa, all of it written by Dad.

During that time there were two official station inspections; each conducted at the Burke residence where the transmitter was located, and where the licence was required to be posted along with the government broadcasting rules and regulations. Each licence shows the station under the name of Island Radio Company. The Island Radio was the name of a bona fide business and it was required as such to secure a commercial broadcasting licence.

During the first few months of the partnership, major alterations were made to the station. With all the increased activity the Burke household was being disrupted. So, in order to get the transmitter out of the living-room, one of the girls' bedrooms was commandeered and the transmitter was moved up to the second floor. Jim Gesner, Dad's retail radio competitor, was hired to weld a metal frame. Not only was the station given its own room, but a special entrance to it cut in the side of the house. All this fully involved the efforts of both my father and Walter Burke.

At this time Dad was working on the old 10AS to increase its power. In a letter to the government, dated September 14, 1925, he states "...our present power is very small—20 watts. It will be some months before power is increased to 100."

The power of the transmitter never reached 100 watts, but shortly after this letter was written, Dad had increased it to 50 watts. The time and expense of rebuilding the original 10AS transmitter was borne by Dad.

For a month after the first CFCY licence was granted, the government hounded the partners for broadcasting schedules. Memos went back and forth from the District Office of Marine to the head office in Ottawa:

"We are concerned CFCY is not advising the Department of its plans and schedules..."

"Sorry, Island Radio does not acknowledge requests to send schedules etc..."

The reason the station was delinquent in sending in plans and schedules is simply because they were constantly in the process of being made. Broadcasting in those days was pretty well a hit and miss affair. It was learn as you go on a shoestring. The larger stations like the Canadian National, or those later stations in Montreal or Toronto with large staffs and lots of financial backing could provide regularly scheduled programs, but the small rural operators could not. Most of them had switched from amateur to professional overnight. During the first few months operating within their new status, they were doing exactly as Dad was doing: setting up, remodelling and expanding. And most of them, like Dad and Walter Burke, were broke.

By early 1926, the pressures upon Dad must have been tremendous, and he was doing a fine juggling act to hold everything together. People, generally, were quite critical of him. "You'd think he'd settle down to serious work at his age, instead of fooling around with all that radio stuff," would be a typical remark. To be thought of as "odd" by the neighbours in Prince Edward Island can seriously affect a person unless he is very tough-minded and independent. Dad was certainly both of these. Once he got an idea and was convinced that he was on the right track, nothing would shake him. He was still selling insurance though. That fed the family.

His commitment to the new radio station, however, was total, and he gave it every available hour he could put into it. It and his retail radio business, a full time job in itself, were a hand in glove operation.

When we buy a radio today, we simply plug it in, if it is not battery operated. Back then an aerial and a ground had be to installed. Parts and tubes wore out quickly, and batteries had to be charged. The batteries that powered the radios in those days were large and cumbersome—something about the size of car batteries—with lead plates submerged in acid. People conserved them for special programs. In the country, people saved them especially for the news and for the funeral announcements that followed the news.

Prince Edward Island farmers can be quite inventive and many of them resorted to amazing devices to keep the batteries charged. Preston Rodd, a Harrington farmer actually designed and constructed a windmill from an old First World War aeroplane propeller. Mr. Rodd, who had been a telegram delivery boy when he was 13, had attended classes with Dad at the Y.M.C.A.

In those years Dad found selling was often difficult because many people had unrealistic expectations as to what a radio could do. In one, but not untypical, case after a long drive out to the country and getting everything set up the new owner asked my father:

"Well, now you say I can get anything on that?"

"Sure you just turn the tuner."

"Okay then—get me, 'Lord MacDonald's Reel.'"

This popular piece of music could not instantly be produced, so the sale went sour. Aerial, ground and radio had to be dismantled and taken back to town.

As the sale of radios, and the demand for servicing grew, relations with Rogers Hardware became far too complicated to remain harmonious. Inevitably, connections were severed. I think it was a case of trying to pour new wine into old bottles.

The pressure to quit everything but the insurance business must have been constant. Dad was going on thirty-five and he had a growing family to support. Instead, he moved the radio business to the basement of the insurance offices on Great George Street and operated from there for the next two and a half years.

The biggest contributing factor in the rift between Dad and Rogers Hardware was due to internal problems. The partners running the hardware store were not getting along. The partner who eventually got the upper hand had not taken to Dad from the start—a "young upstart" he called him, and he wanted him out of the building.

"That radio stuff is too damn messy," he would complain. "Doesn't belong here at all. This is a hardware business. No place for all that noise and commotion from that dratted speaker!"

When Dad had eventually moved all his radio parts and the offending loudspeaker, and they were painting the shelves in preparation for replacing hardware items there, the senior partner came along and commanded the workers:

"I want that shelf taken down! That's where that damn loudspeaker of Keith's was. Take it down and be sure you paint over that spot well. I never want to hear about radio again!"

Chapter Five

Hitting
the
High Notes

M y introduction to broadcasting was somewhat catastrophic. In the fall of 1922, as I said before, Dad decided to demonstrate radios at a booth at the annual Charlottetown Exhibition and Agricultural Fair. Most people had never listened to a radio receiver and they thronged around the booth in great numbers. In addition to displaying the radio sets he had assembled, Dad had built a small transmitter so that he could broadcast music from Bayfield Street to the Exhibition about three miles away. Mother manned the booth while Dad, at home with us, played records on the Victrola placed in front of an old carbon mike. Early microphones would not adjust up and down like later models, so Dad brought the Victrola up to meet the mike by setting it on top of a pile of books and boxes. There it stood in the centre of my sister Marianne's bedroom, teetering amidst a spaghetti-like web of criss-crossing wires.

While Dad was playing records, word got to him that quite a crowd had gathered around the booth out at the Exhibition. Curiosity got the better of him, and he decided to go out there and see for himself. Marianne and I had been having a grand time watching Dad all morning—we were helping out. "Girls," he said, "how would you like to run the gramaphone here while I go to the exhibition to see Mother?" Of course we would. I was just nine years old. My sister was five. He went through the procedure of changing the records a couple of times more. Then, satisfied we could handle it, he left.

When Mum learned what we were doing, she was very concerned

about us being on our own. But at Dad's insistence that we were okay, and lulled by the fact that the music was coming through right on cue, she relaxed.

The fascinated crowd shoved each other to get closer to the booth. I can just picture Dad's dark eyes twinkling as he explained to people what was going on. There was nothing he loved better than spreading the gospel of radio.

Back at the house, Marianne and I, delighted at the fine job we were doing, gained in confidence all the time. We put on a particularly fast piece of music and danced to it. Faster and faster we danced around the precariously balanced microphone until—crash! We tripped over the wires. Down came the books, the boxes, the Victrola, and the mike! At the Exhibition booth horrified listeners heard the screech of the needle, the crash, and the screech of the girls. Mother and Dad looked at each other aghast.

"Heavens Keith, what's happened to the children?" she exclaimed.

Horrified, he answered, "What's happened to my transmitter?"

Apart from being frightened, we were no worse for wear. Mother consoled us, Dad reassembled his equipment, and soon everything was back to normal.

My father's passion for radio and his comittment to it was so profound that it pervaded all our lives. It was inevitable that we became a radio family. Our development as children was in sync with the development of CFCY.

Over the next few years, visitors to our house began to notice that we had quite a few kitchen chairs about the place—without backs. They were for the old-time fiddlers. Throughout the years a tradition of old-time fiddling had developed at CFCY starting with a man called Lem Jay and ending with the famous Don Messer and his Islanders.

Lem, CFCY's earliest performer, broadcast from Bayfield Street. His daughter, Mrs. Bruce MacLaren, told me that the most exciting event in Lem's life was going to Charlottetown to play on the radio. Although the distance from Mount Stewart to Charlottetown is only about twenty miles, in the 1920's that distance by rail took three hours, because the railroad on the Island tends to meander through everybody's backyard. The people back then loved the slow journeys. It was a chance to see the countryside and talk to people.

Of course, as they say, everybody on the Island knows everybody else, and if they don't know them personally, they know somebody who

Courtesy of Mrs. Bruce MacLaren

Lem Jay, a judge at the Old Time Fiddling Contests along with Bob Weeks and Al Dowling.

does. Everyone certainly knew Lem Jay, and I imagine a part of the thrill he got coming down to town to play on the radio was the trip on the train. He used to play old time music for the passengers. In the wintertime, Lem, like most people back then, travelled by horse and sleigh along the river ice, but as soon as the ice broke up in the springtime, he took the train.

We'd get Mr. Jay's special chair in from the porch as soon as we knew he was coming. When he played he had a great swing to his bow arm, and he was a vigorous toe-tapper. Eventually he tapped a hole right

43

through our carpet. He developed a technique of making his own accompaniment by striking the lowest strings on the fiddle. Every time the bow went over it, it rang, and it was this ringing tone that marked Lem Jay's unique style.

The fiddling was popular. Later the old-time fiddling champion, Bob Weeks, travelled in regularly from Highfield. Bob brought a group of fiddlers in with him, and there they'd sit in a ring of backless chairs, these men, playing with great concentration, playing music of their own creation, and music which had its beginnings long ago in Ireland, Scotland, Wales, England and France.

During the first six months of CFCY, broadcasting consisted of what became known in the trade as mechanical music: records played in front of a microphone. The only regularly scheduled broadcasting Dad and Walter Burke were doing then was on Sundays. On September 14, 1925, Dad wrote to Alex Sutherland, Director of Radio, Department of Marine, Halifax:

...due to improving our station we are operating Sundays only:
11:00 a.m. Church Services
1:00 p.m. Hotel Victoria Dinner Concert
7:00 p.m. Church Services.
Aside from this—may go on any evening providing suitable material is available.

The morning church service mentioned here was consistently from the Methodist Church which by this time had become Trinity United Church. The evening services were usually from any other denomination that wished to arrange a broadcast. The Victoria Hotel was Charlottetown's finest. It was a common thing for large family groups to go there for dinner after church on Sunday. There was broadcasting done from there. The Casino Orchestra played dinner music. I know it was heard and enjoyed as far away as Hartford, Connecticut because there is a card from a listener who lived there still on file.

In these very early days there were no formalized techniques with regard to style and format. More effort went into making the equipment work than into polish and illusion. The broadcast took place warts and all. There was a consciousness, though, that one should "speak well", whatever that meant.

44

The announcing voice tended to be consciously over-articulated and theatrical. It was, in effect, an attempt to adjust to the equipment and to create the best impression. Many background noises came through unadulterated along with the broadcast. For example, the church broadcasts and those from the Victoria Hotel were carried to the transmitter at Upper Hillsborough Street over the telephone lines. Listeners came to expect to hear as part of the broadcast Dad and Walter Burke conversing back and forth with each other,

"Okay, Walter, we seem to be all set up here fine. Are you receiving me okay?"

"Loud and clear Keith. I think we're all set to go. Right?"

"Stand by then."

All this technical preamble would be in their everyday normal voices, then whomever happened to be announcing would assume his radio voice.

"Good afternoon. This is radio station CFCY, Charlottetown, Prince Edward Island broadcasting."

It was all very experimental. There was one program, though, which became a part of Walter Burke's devotional hour on Wednesday evenings. Up the street from Burke's lived the Rev. Ewan MacDougall. He was invited to come down to the Burke home to give an inspirational talk. Mail came in from the New England States and from along the Gaspe Coast. The Rev. MacDougall's talks were so popular that Dad arranged for him to broadcast from his own parlour through a telephone line.

Broadcasting from the Burke living-room as I have said, must have caused a great deal of inconvenience at times. They were a large family—four girls and one boy. When the transmitter was moved to its own room upstairs, it relieved some of that pressure. But a new problem was created. There was not enough room for the more sophisticated type of program expected from them. A proper studio was needed, but that would mean a lot of money, and the major alterations to the Burke house to move the transmitter to the second floor had depleted finances. Walter did not want to get any farther in over his head. As far as he was concerned they had done enough. But on the other hand, Dad was champing at the bit to expand. They found a temporary solution. They would broadcast from our living-room on Bayfield Street through telephone hookup. When this decision was made, evening broadcasts became more and more frequent.

What a rush of preparation there was to make ready for them. Everybody was expected to help out. My job was to plug the doorbell and to make sure the telephone was off the hook; Marianne and Bill fetched and carried things. Mother assembled artists, and designed and wrote programs.

Dad's big worry was combatting vibration and echo. If there was too much vibration or echo, or if a singer prolonged a high note, or sang too loudly, the station would go off the air. Or worse, one of the precious tubes might shatter.

As a consequence the walls were draped with bedclothes. Down puffs, patchwork quilts and woolen blankets adorned the walls during broadcasts. The piano in particular gave a lot of trouble because of the vibration of its strings. If it was not completely cocooned in bedding and moved to the centre of the living-room, its notes sounded mushy. Often during a broadcast a new echo would develop, and there would be a frantic but hushed scurry for yet another blanket. The microphone too had to be muffled. It stood there, its round face atop its sturdy brass stand, sporting a child's red stocking cap. We children did not mind in the least giving up our bedclothes. It was fun, exciting, and it meant staying up later.

To accommodate those on our street who did not yet own radios, Dad rigged a loudspeaker outside the house. I can see it yet, the big old-fashioned black horn resting on the window sill with the window jammed down on its neck to keep it in place. A rug was stuffed in the window opening to keep out the street noises. Outside crowds of spell-bound neighbours came out of their houses to listen.

In all of these goings on, Dad benefited greatly from Mother's devo-tion, uniqueness and talents. She was a woman of formidable energy, will and passion which she channeled through a deep love of music. My mother was brought up in a strict Methodist Victorian home in a large family. Grandfather Smith was a Clerk of the County Court and his salary was a modest one. She was taught music by the church organ-ist and we know she passed with honours the Senior Victoria College exams sent from London, England. I am sure had she been given the encouragement which she gave, with great zeal, to my brother Bill, Horace MacEwen, and to other young musicians, she might have gone far as a musical performer.

Be that as it may, she did the very best she could to foster music in herself and in the community. For years she was the organist for Zion

Presbyterian Church, diligently stretching whatever she earned to help keep the house going during lean times. She helped to organize the music festivals which came to play such an important part in Island life, and later she played a major role in helping to organize the Women's Music Club and the Community Concert series on Prince Edward Island. She befriended artists, encouraged them, and blossomed in their company.

Canada owes a debt to women of my Mother's ilk. They laid the foundations of the arts in Canada as we know them today. While men generally took on the role of building the nation's trade, commerce and industry, women voluntarily fostered music, drama and art. It is not surprising then that mother assumed the role of musical authority in Dad's early broadcasts.

One person who featured very strongly in these early broadcasts throughout 1926-1928 was Miss Kathleen Hornby, a well-known violinist and music teacher who launched many on a musical career. She was very versatile and was equally at home playing dance music or light classical selections with her younger sister, Eleanor, or with Mother. Each week The Guardian would write an account of the programs:

The radio program broadcast last evening by CFCY, the Island Radio Company Station, was received clearly in Charlottetown and vicinity at least, many telephone calls being received at the Station and Studio during and after the program.

Miss Kathleen Hornby, violinist, played several selections among which were Souvenir and Serenade by Drdla, which were beautifully rendered and elicited particular mention from the many members of the radio audience. Several duets were rendered by Miss Kathleen Hornby and her younger sister, Miss Eleanor, aged eleven years, were particularly enjoyed and among those may be particularly mentioned, Moonlight and Roses by Lemare and Melody in F by Rubenstein.

The agriculture talk given by Mr. Walter Shaw of the Provincial Department of Agriculture, was very interesting and instructive, and was particularly well-delivered.

47

*These programs being broadcast every Wednesday and
Thursday evening by Mr. Walter Burke and Island Radio
Company, are a practical demonstration of the great value of
a powerful radio station from a publicity angle.*

It was also from Bayfield Street in 1925 that I did my first children's
broadcast. I had forgotten about this until I discovered an old schedule
in the National Archives which mentioned that stories for children would
be read at six-thirty on Thursday evenings. I was twelve at the time and
in Miss Mary Irving's grade seven class at Prince Street School. It was
simply a voice reading a ten minute story. We did not know then how
to add music and sound effects.

Those who performed on early radio—especially concert singers—
risked their reputations. Friends invariably told them that they couldn't
recognize their voices. I remember the night when Hermina West
Richards, a former concert singer possessed of a glorious soprano voice,
was to perform. Mrs. Richards, formerly from Alsace-Lorraine, had
been a protégé and subsequently an understudy of the famous Mme
Ernestine Schumann-Heink, a leading contralto of the Metropolitan
Opera in New York.

Mrs. Richards was not a stereotype of the heavy-busted, over-
bearing prima donna. She was a slender, golden-haired beauty, very
gracious and of regal bearing. She had married an Islander and left the
lights and luminaries of New York to live in Charlottetown. She and
mother became close friends and were to give many recitals together.
Because of her background she was the subject of legend and
speculation—one being, that she could actually shatter wine glasses
with a high "C".

On the evening she was to perform there was much tension. It was
her first time on radio. Dad fretted about the possibility of her high notes
and marvellous vibrato shattering the tubes and knocking out the station.
Mother was determined that nothing should mar the great professional's
first appearance before the microphone, and Mrs. Richards was worried
in case she would make a poor impression on the listeners. After all,
our quilt-padded living-room with its network of wires leading to and
from the stocking-capped microphone was a far cry from the New York
Metropolitan Opera House.

Hermina West Richards.

Avoiding Mother's dark admonishing looks, Dad quietly and deferentially, spoke to the soprano.

"Hermina, when you are approaching a high note would you please back slowly away from the microphone; and then, just when you are about to hit it, please turn your back and sing your note into that far corner." She consented graciously and gave Dad one of her beautiful smiles.

"Two minutes to go." Dad said. As he counted the seconds, the children, Marianne, Bill and I looking through the stair rails in the hall hugged ourselves in expectation.

"...four...three...two...one...We're on the air."

And we were!

49

When it came time for the famous big note, beads of sweat stood out on Dad's brow. He held the controls. She held the note, and we held our breath. The needle on the control panel wobbled... wobbled... HELD. Everyone let out a sigh. We had won. The station was still on the air. Dad beamed, and when the soprano turned around he silently took her hand and bowed to her.

With Mother playing quiet music on the piano, Dad signed off. The crowd outside on the street applauded and slowly drifted away. The excitement was over. As soon as they were taken down off the walls, Marianne scooped up her own and Bill's blankets and down puffs, and the two sleepy children stumbled off to bed.

Chapter Six

The Glorious
Confederation
Broadcast

After Dad left Roger's Hardware, he moved his operation to the basement of the "W.K.'s" insurance offices. He was literally swamped with work. One particularly harried day, while loading his large, old Studebaker with radio receivers for delivery, he noticed he had a flat tire. For some reason changing it gave him a lot of trouble.

"Here, sir, let me help you", a polite voice said.

The voice belonged to that of a wirey, bright-looking young teenager called Tony Shelfoon. Once the tire had been changed, the two stood and chatted. Dad was impressed with the young man's charm and obvious intelligence. He learned, too, that Tony had a keen interest in wireless and, indeed, knew a fair bit about electricity and radio. When Dad asked him where he learned so much, he told him that when he was younger he used to hang around Bayfield Street hoping to catch a glimpse of him setting up the apparatus.

"You probably don't remember, Mr. Rogers, but I spoke to you one day and asked you what you were doing. And you replied, "Well, I'm preparing to communicate with the world through wireless-telegraphy." It made me want to learn more about it, so I did."

Dad realized he was speaking to a gifted and highly intelligent young man, which, of course, he was. In later life Tony rose to the rank of Air Commodore in the Royal Air Force and Royal Canadian Air Force. He was decorated, and in the final stage of his career was director

Courtesy of George Shelfoon

Queen Elizabeth II inspecting bomber base,
England 1942. Air Commodore Alan Shelfoon
(rt.)

of some sensitive defence work in Canada, Great Britain, and the United States.

Tony became a general helper, Dad got him an old jalopy. I think it was a little Ford panel truck, to go around installing batteries, aerials, and radios. Frequently, though, there would be pretty girls riding around as well.

On Brighton Road, in Charlottetown, there was a popular dancehall,

Foster's, with a "hot" band, the term in those days for a good, upbeat, jazz dance-band. It was a favourite haunt of the young people, and of course, Tony's. Dad learned that Tony used to take the little truck there. One night when the dance was over, Tony found a note on the truck in Dad's handwriting.

"I'm tired of you leaving me out in the street all night. Please take me home. I have to go to work in the morning."

As I have mentioned, Dad had broadcast from Rogers Hardware until 1924 to make the radios he was selling more attractive to buyers. Aside from what he put on the air, there wasn't much they could receive during the daylight hours. Now that he was out of the hardware store, the afternoon broadcasts had ceased again, and he was quite concerned about this. The CFCY transmitter was broadcasting some evenings in addition to the regular church services and the dinner programs from the Victoria Hotel. Dad was anxious to expand the programming. To achieve this he was beginning to try more sophisticated programming from our living-room. But listeners could still receive very little during the day.

There were so many problems militating against him. The basement of the insurance office was not suitable. The transmitter was at Burke's on Upper Hillsboro Street and Walter Burke was working at Carter's during the day. Dad had to sell insurance during the day. The embryonic industry of broadcasting was demanding more room to grow.

Money was not plentiful. I think at this point in 1927, Dad realized that now was the time to either stay in broadcasting or to get out of it. If he opted to stay, more capital and time were needed. The insurance business fed the family; the retail radio business, if expanded, might provide the capital for an enlarged broadcasting operation. The Bayfield Street broadcasts with their successful use of local talent seemed to point the way to a promising future. He chose to stay in broadcasting. Unconsciously, of course, events and circumstances had been pushing him along in that direction anyway.

He realized that if he were to continue to sell radios he needed a more formal arrangement than the basement of the insurance building. So he made what was to become a well beaten path to the bank manager and arranged the backing to buy more stock and to rent a little place on Kent Street, Charlottetown. This little store was situated on the site where the new Veterans Affairs building now stands. Tony Shelfoon did the broadcasting and selling, while Angus MacMaster built radios and Dad concentrated on insurance and the very nascent CFCY.

At this stage there was no formal transmitter at the Kent Street store. The transmitter at Upper Hillsborough Street was unavailable during the day. So in order to put something over the air during the daytime, they improvised by cleverly maladjusting a radio receiver so that it sent out a signal instead of receiving one.

The afternoon "programmes" went out under the call letters CFCY. I say programs in quotes because there was no formal or planned program at all. Tony had the choice of playing a flat disk wind-up gramaphone, or an old wax cylinder Edison-Ediphone, depending on which was the more interesting. The microphone consisted of a converted earpiece of an old headset which was suspended in front of whichever happened to be playing—the gramaphone or the Ediphone.

Tony's interest, of course, lay in jazz. Jazz in those days was about as obnoxious to the older generation as heavy rock would be to most seniors today. Tony, much to the delight of the younger set, loved to play the "hot" numbers. One lunch time he was playing the "latest" when Dad rushed into the store and whipped off the offensive record and smashed it. "Damn it Tony," he said, "I don't mind you playing your infernal noise at times, but not at mealtimes! You just can't eat soup in time to a fox-trot. It's uncivilized."

This was the "studio". Again I say studio advisedly because the shop, office and studio were all the same thing. They tried to cut down exterior noise by tenting the mike and record-player with a coat or a blanket, but the hiss of the needle drowned out the music. They just let it go in the end. If Tony was playing something over the air and a customer came in, he waited on them and their conversation went over the air too.

Tony recalled later during a trip to Charlottetown that one of the things that stayed with him was Dad's insistence on the use of proper language:

"The search for the right word and its pronunciation developed in me a feel for language. I didn't get into what was considered

*real announcing until Keith got laryngitis and he asked me to
do a program from Bayfield Street. Mrs. Rogers was playing
the piano and one of the local belles was singing. It was so dark
in the drawing-room I could hardly read the notes. Mrs. Rogers
was to play a Rachmaninov prelude. I pronounced it Ratch-ee-
man-off, but I was gently set straight. Keith Rogers was a kindly
mentor."*

In 1927, there was a rather elaborate plan by Ottawa for broadcasting the Sixtieth Anniversary ceremonies of the Canadian
Confederation.

Whether it was because the hard-headed Islanders had refused to
come into Confederation until 1873 or not, I'll never know. But CFCY,
the only broadcasting station on Prince Edward Island, was completely
excluded from the original plans to feed the broadcast from coast to
coast. Islanders were told that if they wanted to hear the mammoth
broadcast by the special national network—a broadcast which would
make world history because it was to cover the sheer vastness of
Canada—they had to tune into the 500 watt Canadian National Railway
Station transmitter, CNRA, Moncton. Dad was incensed. He saw the
exclusion both as a personal slight, and as an insult to the Island. Letters
flew back and forth.

"Was not Prince Edward Island the Cradle of Confederation? Why
then exclude it when facilities are here capable and ready to participate?" he asked. But the organizing committee reiterated its stand, as
though there was nothing further to be said in the matter. Its constant
reply was, "...although it seems facilities are definitely available, there
would, however, be no extension of the regular network."

Little did they know who they were dealing with. Dad's gentle
manner masked a streak of stubborness which when aroused made him
a formidable foe. More letters were exchanged, but still the same tire-
some reply came back from Ottawa. Undaunted, Dad researched how
the Diamond Jubilee broadcast would actually be managed. He learned
that the program, though taking place in Ottawa, was to be beamed by
shortwave from the Marconi station in Drummondville, Quebec to
England for rebroadcast. For several days he monitored the
Drummondville frequency and concluded that he would get a better
reception for the Ottawa broadcast by shortwave than from the regular

network which came via the Borden-Tormentine cable, and which, after it reached Borden, would have to be transmitted through the iron telegraph wire of the Canadian National Telegraph.

After clearly stating his findings, Dad reasoned that for him to receive the broadcast directly from Drummondville he would not, in any way, be interfering with the committee's planning and would not be "...causing an extension to the regular network." To reinforce CFCY's position, Mr. Justice Arsenault, the local Chairman, wired the central committee for its permission for CFCY to rebroadcast from Drummondville.

Commander Edwards, Director of the Radio Division of the Department of Transport, and Chairman of the Central Committee on Broadcasting, had had enough. Exasperated, he wired back to Justice Arsenault:

TELL THAT MAN ROGERS TO DO WHAT HE DAMN WELL PLEASES STOP

That was all Dad needed.

His company, the *Royal Corps of Signals*—"Roger's Rangers" as it was known locally—was in summer camp at Charlottetown's Victoria Park. He had technicians on hand ready and willing to gain new experience. They assembled and installed the first public address system ever on Prince Edward Island. It consisted of some 12 powerful Magnavox speakers ranged around what was known as the "cricket field". These faced the "grand stand" or bleachers constructed by the local committee.

When the big day arrived all the local speeches from the VIP rostrum were fed through the loudspeakers, and when the time came for the broadcast, a perfect reception was tuned in from Drummondville which was fed through the address system and through the Island on CFCY. Percival Price played "O Canada" on the Peace Tower Carillon, and a choir of 1,000 school children sang. Of course, there were speeches by Prime Minister MacKenzie King, and the Leader of the Opposition as well as other dignitaries. Throughout the entire proceedings there was nothing to mar the one hundred per cent perfect rebroadcast. For his own satisfaction, Dad monitored the broadcast from

Moncton and found it was so bad, at times, it could not be made out. Hundreds of letters poured into the station from a wide area of listeners lauding CFCY. Dad felt vindicated and proud that the Island received the program perfectly by shortwave from Drummondville, via CFCY.

Chapter Seven

Expansion, Rifts
and
Competition

It soon became apparent that after a year of broadcasting from our living room CFCY was going to have to be on the air more frequently. In order to do this several things were needed: studio facilities, more power, more staff, and, of course, more money. Besides its inconvenient location, the transmitter at Upper Hillsborough Street was too small. For three years now, Walter Burke and Dad had been operating out of their homes—the transmitter in one, and the studio in another more than half a mile away, contact and transmission having to be made by telephone. The afternoon broadcasts from the tiny Kent Street store were too crude. Everything was too makeshift. Although Tony was doing a good job, and his announcing and technical skills were really improving, the store was barely breaking even. Some months, Dad, had a hard time finding the rent after meeting salaries and costs.

In 1926, Dad had written for approval to expand to 100 watts. Permission was granted along with this issuance of the new licence. Under Dad's tutelage, Tony, with his quick mind, was able to assemble a new 100-watt transmitter throughout 1927. The new transmitter completed, Dad logically concluded that if CFCY was to expand properly, transmitter, studio facilities, and store should be consolidated under one roof, which meant a larger location. In January, 1928, he moved to new quarters at 143 Great George Street—now University Avenue.

The new place was a shop with a large display window and long narrow store space inside. Attached to the back was a low shed area for storage which he partitioned to serve as a studio and control room.

The building is still there today housing a fashionable ladies clothing store. Dad remained at Great George Street for seven years — the formative years of broadcasting on Prince Edward Island.

In the meantime, Walter Burke was holding back on expansion. The new 100-watt transmitter that Tony Shelfoon had been working on was nearing completion. CFCY had become a well known station around the Maritimes — indeed for many places it was the only station. Dad tried to persuade Mr. Burke to move the old transmitter, the original 10AS, down to Great George Street to incorporate it with the new 100-watt transmitter. But Mr. Burke would not budge. He felt it was his station and that it should stay exactly where it was. For the last three years, Dad had been paying for the licence under the name of the Island Radio Company. He did this with the full knowledge and agreement of Mr. Burke, because the licence was required to be displayed in the station beside the transmitter. And the station had received three official inspections from the Department of Marine, Radio Division, by the Government Inspector, Electrician H. A. Coade.

My father was spending more and more time running the affairs of CFCY. Walter Burke was finding it difficult to do any radio work in the day time as he had a fulltime job at Carter and Company and a large family to support. He felt he could not take the risk of leaving his position. Furthermore, his ideas for building up the radio station differed from Dad's. Walter wanted to have the transmitter at his home to use after work and for broadcasting the church services, but my father was contemplating a community radio station eventually broadcasting most of the daytime and evening hours. Relations became strained, and the two friends found they could no longer see eye to eye on even the most fundamental changes.

The Department of Marine, Radio Division would not allow them to use two transmitters in different locations under the same call letters. In the daytime my father was using the call letters CFCY — call letters he had applied for, paid for, for three years, and received from the department. That meant that if Walter Burke wanted to use his transmitter on Hillsboro street, he would have to apply for a new licence with new call letters.

For whatever reason, Mr. Burke neglected to apply for the new call letters. The dispute flared into anger. Mr. Burke felt that my father had been unfair to him, and he engaged a lawyer. In the lawyer's office both men sorted out their affairs. It was decided that because of the amount

59

of work Dad had done on the expansion of the transmitter and because of the equipment he had bought to put into it, each of them owned half the transmitter. It was also decided that my father would give Walter Burke the entire proceeds of a series of political broadcasts to be done over the Hillsboro Street transmitter and with this money, Walter would buy my father's share of the transmitter, and own it completely. My father was to keep on paying for and using the call letters CFCY, and to make no objection to another licence being granted in the city. As far as Dad was concerned the matter was settled, and he felt he had been fair in dealing with Mr. Burke and his lawyer. All he wanted to do was attend to his own business and try to make a success of it.

Looking at all of the correspondence, it seems to me it was a fair arrangement, fairly arrived at.

When the split finally came between Mr. Burke and Dad, Dad felt very badly about it. He felt he had no choice. He had bought the licences for three years, had supplied all the technical expertise had written all the correspondence between the station and Ottawa, and had designed and put together the bulk of the programming which for two years had originated mainly from our living room on Bayfield Street. He had engineered and fought single-handedly for the broadcast of the Jubilee Celebrations, not to mention other important events like political rallies.

It was time for expansion. His letterhead for three years had read the Island Radio Company, Station CFCY, Charlottetown. He saw no reason to change now after all his work and expense.

In 1928, however, when Mr. Burke and Dad finally separated, Mr. Burke was still very upset. Mutual friends tried to bring the two men together to see if they could work something out. It would appear they actually attempted to do this, because in the National Archives there is a letter from my Dad with a cheque requesting the 1928 CFCY licence be issued under the joint ownership of Walter E. Burke and Keith S. Rogers, address 143 Great George Street. But something happened. What it was we will never know. We can only surmise that the two men once again disagreed, because another letter was sent off requesting joint ownership, but this time listing **two** transmitters, one at Upper Hillsboro Street, Burke's and the other located at 143 Great George Street, Dad's. This request was turned down and the partnership broke up. Eventually the former cheque was returned to Dad and a new licence was issued to Island Radio, CFCY, 143 Great George Street.

Walter Hyndman, who was Radio Inspector for the area at the time,

60

advised Walter Burke to apply for a new licence. He did, and was granted the call letters CHCK. Unfortunately Walter Burke was no technician. He could operate the transmitter but he did not understand technical matters beyond a certain point and needed someone with that ability to keep the station on the air.

A radio station is its hardware such as the transmitter, the studio and its equipment, the real estate, and all the administration and talent that goes along with it. The call letters of a station such as CFCY, CHCK, CFRB etc., are merely the government's official designation of that station. The station on Upper Hillsborough Street which had formerly been designated CFCY, now became CHCK when Mr. Burke, on Walter Hyndman's advice, applied for and was granted a new licence. From 1928, the call letters CFCY officially designated Dad's new 100 watt station on Kent street. Charlottetown from that point onward had two official commercial broadcasting stations.

When Mr. Burke applied for another commercial licence, Dad was asked by Ottawa if he had any objections. Convinced Mr. Burke wished nothing more than to do his Wednesday evening program of sacred and classical music and to broadcast church services on Sundays, he responded that he had no objections whatsoever.

Another factor, however, entered into the situation. James A. Gesner, Dad's chief competitor in the retail radio business offered to take Dad's place to do the technical work on the transmitter in order to keep it on the air and to make the business arrangements as Mr. Burke was busy at Carter & Co. Although there is no actual written proof, I have learned that there was a small, silent coterie of political and business friends in the background allied to Jim Gesner. When Gesner entered the scene, the stew was on the stove—a stew given its flavour by the ingredients of a dash of politics, the personalities of the competitors, the business element itself, and, not to mention of course, the amusing distractions it provided for the neighbouring downtown merchants and sometimes for the listeners. The combatants, like most men when they get stubborn and squabble, acted many times like schoolboys giving the competition that evolved between them a humourous side to it.

Charlottetown then just wasn't big enough to support two commercial stations; and besides that, broadcasting in Canada was under review. The Aird Commission was holding meetings throughout the country. The Canadian Radio Broadcasting Commission network was soon to

61

be born, and those stations throughout the country selected to be officially made a part of it would have a promising future in Canadian broadcasting. My father always kept in touch with an old friend Major William C. Borrett of Halifax, a pioneer in broadcasting in Nova Scotia (CHNS licenced in 1926). They worked together with others to promote chain broadcasting as it was called then.

In PEI the station chosen would either be CFCY or CHCK or CHGS in Summerside (licence granted 1927 with a power of 25 watts.)

Ottawa aggravated the competition by making the Charlottetown stations share the same wavelength. The broadcasting day was divided between them and in many a game of tit for tat, listeners would hear God Save The King blending discordantly with O Canada as one station signed off perhaps late, or the other signed on too early. Mr. Gesner at CHCK would retaliate by breaking in on the middle of CFCY's broadcasts with "CHCK Testing. CHCK Testing." Fist shaking and insults would be hurled across the street. One old timer recalls my father brandishing a tire-iron.

Accusatory letters flew back and forth to Ottawa—"Rogers is telling his customers that only his stock can be guaranteed as fresh and good", or, "We obey the government regulations, why cannot Gesner and CHCK be made to do the same?" Gesner, with the backing of the Marconi Company, built up a case against Dad accusing him of direct advertising which was forbidden in those years. Ottawa responded by revoking Dad's permission to advertise his retail products directly over the air. **Round to Gesner**.

Dad got on the air and asked for support from listeners. Letters poured in from around the Maritimes and these were sent to Ottawa. Ottawa wrote Gesner saying his reports were exaggerated. **Round for Dad**.

More support was solicited by both competitors over the air. Complaints ranging from trivial to serious were made almost daily. There were signed petitions from citizens, and letters from politicians— the local liberals backing one station, local Conservatives the other. Inter office memoranda from senior civil servants to juniors asked for and gave clarification. Even government station inspectors at times seemed to take sides because on a few occasions they added their personal opinions, for which they received a ticking off by their supervisors:

...it is not your business to comment one way or the other in this matter. It is the policy of the Department to remain impartial in disputes of this nature. The station owners must come to some agreement themselves.

It lasted for ten years, causing considerable distress to the opponents—especially for Mr. Burke. My father was upset because Walter Burke was caught in the middle; and he was distressed because of the frustration and energy which had to be expended. But a battle is a battle and must be fought to be won. Jim Gesner was as tenacious as Dad until he later left the Island. The alignments and realignments of sides in this struggle were like a microcosm of world powers in their perpetual struggle to seek a balance of power. What it amounted to in the end, was in the best tradition of North American free enterprise— there had to be a winner and there had to be a loser and in the interim, there was a vigorous scrap.

In the last analysis, it came down to a competition between Jim Gesner and my Dad, Mr. Burke really having no taste for it. A devoted family man, a hard worker, and a devout Methodist churchman, Mr. Burke was well regarded by the many who knew him. The words of Joe Rodd, the retired owner of Toombs Music Store in Charlottetown, typify the general opinion of him:

"Burke was a man you couldn't discourage—he'd come up smiling. It was his religion. He was a very religious man—Oh not the book kind, he carried it far beyond. You couldn't get a more honest, kinder man".

Mr. Burke's association with Gesner lasted more or less about three years and deteriorated steadily over the next four. The quality of the progamming deteriorated to nothing more than that played over a gramaphone—or mechanical music as it was called then. In addition to sacred music the only other kind Mr. Burke considered in good taste was light classical, and when these gave way more and more to raucous popular hits and jazz played over the phonograph, he protested; but

63

when the Sunday broadcasts from his beloved Trinity Church were neglected, he was appalled.

Gesner, through political pull it was suggested, received the franchise to broadcast the local hockey games from the Charlottetown Forum, and these took precedence over everything else. As far as Mr. Burke was concerned, the sacred—his reason for getting into broadcasting in the first place—had been superseded by the profane. Mr. Burke was distraught. The CHCK transmitter, the old 10AS, was still located in the second story of the Burke home, and as long as it was there, Walter had a measure of control. However, one afternoon, Mr. Gesner went to the Burke home in the daytime when Walter was at work and took the transmitter to his downtown office, almost directly across the street from Dad's Great George Street studio. Walter Burke's files were missing and from then on he was practically denied access to them.

Mr. Burke could see nothing but increasing trouble ahead from his association with Gesner and CHCK. Gesner was in financial trouble and Walter Burke did not want to be held responsible for Mr. Gesner's debts. Eventually he appealed to Dad to take over the Church broadcasts. They patched up their differences and Mr. Burke, wanting to get out of a bad mess, sold Dad his half interest in CHCK. Now this entire issue had never really been properly addressed so I would like to reproduce now two documents in full from the files of the National Archives in Ottawa.

"For One Dollar, to me in hand, together with other valuable considerations, I Walter E. Burke, of Charlottetown, the Province of Prince Edward Island Canada, do hereby transfer to Keith Sinclair Rogers of Charlottetown, Prince Edward Island, all of my right title and interest in the licence to operate station CHCK, issued jointly in the name of Walter E. Burke and James A. Gesner together with my interest in the transmitting apparatus, record library and other machinery employed in the operation of said radio station CHCK and delegate to the said Keith Sinclair Rogers the right to protect his interest in the said Broadcasting Station Licence, issued by the Department of Marine, Ottawa, in the way he may deem necessary.

I, Walter E. Burke, of Charlottetown, P.E. Island do hereby make this full and complete assignment of my interest in the said Radio Station CHCK to the said Keith S. Rogers of Charlottetown and declare the same binding in every way upon myself and upon my legal heirs and assigns.

Dated at Charlottetown, P.E.I.
June 20, 1936.

Witness: Billy Warren   *Signed: Walter E. Burke*
                                            K.S. Rogers.

My father has been accused of treating Walter Burke in a shabby manner—a residue, no doubt, from this competition for radio dominance in Charlottetown. But this was not the case and I offer the following document from Mr. Burke's own hand:

To Whom it May Concern:—

I wish to make it a matter of record that in all business dealings with Keith S. Rogers, in connection with Radio Broadcasting, or other matters, in particular with our association prior to 1928 in the operation of Radio Station CFCY and its affairs, I have always found Mr. Rogers to be fair and honourable in every way. I wish further to state that in the dissolution of our association in 1928, for the operation of CFCY, Mr. Rogers assisted me in many ways that he was not obliged to take but were of considerable assistance to me in establishing CHCK on my own behalf. I wish further to state that in the breaking up of our association together in the operation of CFCY prior to 1928, Mr. Rogers treated me in an eminently fair and just manner and to my complete satisfaction.

Dated at Charlottetown, P.E.I.

May 17th, 1936   *Signed: Walter E. Burke.*

Ironically, the dissolution of the Gesner-Burke association left the two arch enemies, Rogers and Gesner, CFCY and CHCK, in dubious partnership—strange bedfellows, indeed.

Ottawa, before granting a new licence to Gesner, wished to know the details of his partnership with Mr. Burke. There is no record of Mr. Gesner's reply, but there does exist a letter from Mr. Burke denying that anything like a formal partnership ever existed between himself and Mr. Gesner, other than a working association. Eventually Jim Gesner was placed in a position of operating CHCK illegally. Dad had bought Walter Burke's interests in the licence and in the studio and transmission equipment. When it came time to re-licence CHCK Dad refused to have anything to do with Gesner. It was a fait accompli. Gesner was faced with the prospect of starting fresh with an entirely new station and making application for yet another licence. In the interim, CFCY had become part of the new Canadian Radio Broadcasting Commission network. James Gesner left the Island soon after this and Dad purchased his shares and the shares of the board of directors of the Gesner station. CHCK had played an important part in the history of broadcasting in Prince Edward Island.

Chapter Eight

"Where
The
Boys Meet!"

It was the custom of Islanders in those days to come into town on Saturdays to do their shopping. Their day began early at the Farmer's Market which was located on the site where the Confederation Center of the Arts now stands. Throughout the rest of the day people poured steadily in and out of town until the stores closed at nine o'clock in the evening. Most of the retail businesses in those days before shopping malls and chain stores were located right in the centre of town in a block facing the Farmer's Market, and surrounded by Kent, Queen, Grafton and Great George Streets. There were more horses and buggies than cars being used then, and livery stables were more in use than garages. The area I'm talking about was nicknamed Dizzy Block because it was the custom for the people to walk around and around it. Friends and relatives from different parts of the Island would meet and catch up with the latest news and gossip; and, of course, it was a good place for boys and girls to meet.

Dad's store and studio was a very popular stopping place. People were encouraged to participate if they had talent to offer. You got to the studio by going through the store to the converted shed out back. Probably one of the smallest studios ever, it housed an old upright piano, a microphone and as many chairs as could be squeezed in. There were no windows, just a tiny peep-hole in the door and a glass panel to the control room. The walls and ceiling were completely covered with an inexpensive soundproofing board material that unfortunately gave out a musty odour like the lingering smell of boiled cabbage when the temperature and humidity were high, which was generally the case.

The small control room housed the transmitter and the latest invention for broadcasting, studio turntables. Gone was the old gramaphone in front of the microphone. Those in the store could listen to the broadcast over one or more of the radios on sale there, while those in the street could hear it from the loudspeaker over the door.

CFCY transmitter and control console 1927.

People walking around the "dizzy block" would be startled to hear the deep BONG, BONG, BONG—the chimes of London's Big Ben resounding up and down the street peeling out midnight even though it would only be eight o'clock in Prince Edward Island.

During these evenings all the talent was local, live, and unrehearsed. The performers may have rehearsed at home, but once they got into the studio, they were put right "on the air!"

After the move to Great George Street, the broadcasts from Bayfield Street had dwindled rapidly. One of the last involved Horace MacEwen playing a piano recital, and a newly-arrived couple from Geneva,

Switzerland, Marguerite and Raoul Reymond, who sang in French a program of classical music. They would later be among my father and mother's dearest friends. The Jubilee Celebrations had made Dad realize just how much scope he had if he could pick up short wave transmission. So throughout the rest of 1928, there were many rebroadcasts from Eindhoven, Holland; Nausen, Germany; and from the Eiffel Tower in Paris. Events closer to home were also broadcast by remote control like the anniversary church services of a church in Westville, Nova Scotia.

There was a long tradition on the Island of local talent expressing itself at parties, concerts, and dances in the community halls. A community would organize its best talent and visit a neighbouring hall. These events were known as "times". People were very proud of their community, and there was a fair bit of competition. When radio came in, it was a source of pride if someone from one's community was on the air. In a sense, early CFCY broadcasting was like one great big Island hall. People felt free to drop in off the street and entertain a little, lending a party atmosphere to the broadcasts.

Take Frank "Duck" Acorn, for example, who used to broadcast at the noon hour from great George Street along with his friend Bill MacEachern. It seems that so many people in those years made a lot of music together, spontaneously. "Duck" learned to play from a man named Ed Garnhum who was an inveterate ukulele player. Ed worked for Henderson and Cudmore, the haberdashery. Apparently, Ed never stopped playing, even while working. They say that when he would be carrying parcels out of the store to deliver, he would have the uke slung over his back, and as soon as he got rid of the parcels, he'd play his ukulele as he walked along the street back to the store.

"Duck" Acorn's father owned a restaurant on Great George Street. Its slogan was "Where the Boys Meet!" and indeed they did—to make music. There was Holly Warren and his brother Monty, Percy Steele, Ed Acorn and his two brothers, and Bill MacEachern, who was a superb mouth organist and singer. All of them were avid musicians, and they had what they called their "orchestra" which was an assortment of guitars, banjos, ukes, fiddles, mouth organs, and, of course, voice. Dad would get Tony Shelfoon to go down to the restaurant to put them on a telephone line to the transmitter and they would go over the air extemporaneously. Everybody knew them and loved them.

Later when Dad was at Great George Street, CFCY used to join the American Relay League DX program after midnight as a means of seeing how far away the station could be heard. This same gang would move down to the studio from the restaurant and play and sing for the test until the "wee" hours. Today, of course, this would be done using a recording, but in those days at CFCY it was an occasion for a party.

"Duck" Acorn and Billy MacEachern worked so well as a pair, and were so popular around the Island, that Dad got them to broadcast at noontime. They were merely teenagers, and because they didn't believe they were all that good, they were reluctant to give their names out over the air. But most people knew who they were anyway. Dad gave them the team name of "Duck and Bill."

They got into the station at noon and waited around until Dad finished waiting on a customer, or got off the phone. Between selling radios and insurance he was kept busy and did a lot of business over the telephone. Usually he'd just thumb them through to the back, and when he got a breather he'd go back to the studio and announce them. Throughout the program, Duck and Bill and whoever would be operating, would be left to their own devices if Dad continued to be tied up—that is how free-wheeling things were in those days.

Apparently Billy, who was blind, rocked back and forth when he sang. It was his way of keeping time. Dad got him an old rocking chair that squeaked, or else the floor did, or both. Anyhow, the squeak went over the air and seemed to fit the act as an extra instrument, almost. That steady squeak-squeak beat gave them a great sense of timing and added an extra kick to their theme song, "The Big Rock Candy Mountain."

Another noon-time program I remember, was The Home Forum produced by CFCY's first woman free-lance broadcaster "Flo" Fitzgerald. Starting in the early thirties, it ran for seventeen years. Mrs. Fitzgerald—who very early worked in sales and production—was original, inventive and creative. When she signed up a chicken canning firm, she told her sons Bill and Babs to learn how to cackle like hens and crow like roosters. There were no tape recorders then, and they were on "live" each time "The Hen Party" was broadcast. The boys were so good everyone was convinced there were real hens in the studio. Flo had a way of picking out items that would interest the communities along the north shore of Nova Scotia as well as her home province, and she would sell, announce and produce her own program.

Flora Hope Wiggins Fitzgerald was born and brought up on a farm in Darnley, P.E.I. Her manners were impeccable and she was very strict about the use of proper English. This attention to detail came from her uncle Sir Louis Henry Davies who was Chief Justice for Canada. We all knew that we must observe the proprieties when she was around, and I must say that she was very gentle as she pointed out mistakes made on the air.

Flo was witty and she wrote and directed for the "CFCY Players". The sponsor was Hyndman & Co. advertising fire insurance. One night my father, who was announcing the show, tapped his pipe out on the side of the waste basket setting the whole thing aflame. He was reading the announcement about fire insurance at the time. Grabbing one of the fire extinguishers which fortunately we happened to be selling in the radio shop, Les Peppin doused the fire. The play never faltered, no lines were lost.

Courtesy of T.L. Fitzgerald

"Flo" Fitzgerald, CFCY's first woman free-lance broadcaster.

My father and Mrs. Fitzgerald got along famously. she had been on the air many years when she thought up the idea of selling goodwill advertising at Christmas. She told not a soul but bought an hour from Dad for Christmas Day. He was extremely busy and didn't ask her what she was going to do with it. When she came back for another hour, he still neglected to ask although he was curious. When she requested a third hour, he sold it to her for New Year's Day. It was then that he woke up to the realization that this tiny older lady had scooped the sales staff and sold out three solid hours. He called together Art McDonald and those connected with sales and gave them an intense lecture on the necessity of keeping abreast of the times. He rammed home the message that they should get out into the community and really go to work. As he left the room, he could barely suppress a chortle.

Like most people in radio, Flo had her bloopers. The LePage Shoe Store received a new shipment of galoshes. It was during the sloppy spring weather. In all innocence she went on air with a commercial warning her customers:

Buy your galoshes today,
Don't get caught up-town
With nothing but your rubbers on!

All day people kept dropping into the sponsor's store, buying the galoshes and laughing their heads off.

Chapter Nine

Sad Fate
of the
Water-cooled Tube

The years at the end of the twenties were high-spirited euphoric times. Well they deserved the name the "Roaring Twenties". Just as the "Sixties" forty years later polarized the values of the younger and older generations, so did the twenties. Sedate Victorians blushed and remonstrated at Charleston kicking, bead-swinging flappers. Jazz blared, drowning out the soft strings of Victor Herbert, and fast cars were pushing horses off the roads back to the confines of the farm. There was prohibition, bathtub gin and gangsters in the United States. On Prince Edward Island there was prohibition too, and rum-runners carried on a lucrative trade with the American underworld. Stockmarket investments were making millionaires—on paper—overnight. Almost everyone with a few dollars to spare was having a flutter on the stockmarket. Talking pictures were making the world laugh and cry on a scale never known before; and, of course, so was radio.

Rural places, such as Prince Edward Island, were having an enormous dint made in their insularity; and as Dad had predicted, the Aladdin's Lamp of radio had opened up a fantasy world of hitherto untold riches and sophistication. A great aping—especially among the young—of opulent classes began to take place as these were presented through the movies and radio. This opulence was represented in many ways, from society chit-chat columns in newspapers and magazines to different kinds of radio programs. In the U.S. many broadcasting companies did remotes from large hotels. Through radio, the ballroom of the Waldorf Astoria and the palm-treed lobby of the Grand Hotel in

New York City were now accessible to the masses wherever they might be.

The broadcasts were so popular that networks around the world imitated them. In Canada, Toronto's King Edward Hotel Ballroom was most popular, followed later by the opulent Royal York. Until as late as the 1960's CFCY carried the very romantic and popular, "Dancing Under the Stars" from Ontario's Brant Inn, Burlington. The Big Band era grew out of this tradition, one of the most nostalgic being Guy Lombardo and his Royal Canadians.

Dad and Walter Burke broadcast their Sunday dinner program from Charlottetown's finest hotel, the Victoria. Dad thought it would be a good idea to build a posh studio there. Mother designed and decorated it. When she was through, it was elegant and in good taste with the walls hung in red velvet drapes and the floor deeply carpeted. The tiny shed at Great George Street with its aged and worn piano was not at all suitable for the classical musical recitals we had broadcast from Bayfield Street. The elegant new studio at the hotel, which sported a very fine piano belonging to my grandmother, was ideal for more sophisticated types of programming. In the fall of 1928 a fashionable concert was given featuring Horace MacEwen on the piano, mother and Mrs. Hermina Richards, and the Casino Orchestra. The Casino was a small string ensemble hired on a regular basis by the hotel. Most of its members were students or former students of Kathleen Hornby.

The Victoria Hotel studio, however, was short lived, for on a November night in 1929, a fire started in the basement of the hotel. The flames shot up the elevator shaft and before the night ended, the entire building was engulfed. With high winds blowing from the harbour, all the fire-fighters could do was prevent the flames from leaping to other buildings. The hotel had just taken in a fresh delivery of coal that day, and apparently this burned and glowed for weeks. Fortunately, there was no loss of life. The Charlottetown Volunteer Fire Brigade did a miraculous job of saving the wooden houses and buildings that make up that part of the city. Only forty years earlier, a great part of Charlottetown had been destroyed in what is now known as the "Great Fire".

Luckily the building was insured, and when Dad moved in there he had put on extra insurance to cover the new studio. The only thing that was not insured was Grandmother's piano, but fortunately it was rescued, unscathed, from the inferno.

Craswell Photo

Orpheus Eight. This group of men entertained all over the Province for thirty years. They were the first to broadcast coast-to-coast from Charlottetown. 1933.
Dr. Earl Robbins, Elmer Dunning, Leigh Dingwell, Frank McDonald, Jack Sterns, Art Bruce, Bill Brennen, Elmer Ritchie.

When Tony Shelfoon left CFCY in 1929, to work in radio in Saint John, New Brunswick, his place was taken by a young sixteen-year-old called Les Peppin. Les was sitting round the house one day waiting for his dinner and listening to the radio when Dad came on with the following announcement:

Wanted: two strong, bright and courteous boys who are not too proud to sweep floors, run errands, and install aerials...We want you to be willing to learn radio from the ground up.

Les shouted to his mother, "Hold my dinner Mom!" He was a keen cyclist and all that summer had been heavily involved in bicycle racing. The city speed limit for cars then was only twelve miles per hour, but Les could do almost thirty miles per hour on his bike. A quarter of a mile later he screeched to a halt in front of 143 Great George Street.

"Is the job still open, sir?" he asked Dad.

"Where did you come from?"

"From down the far end of Euston Street," Les said.

"But I just this minute made the announcement," said Dad, incredulously. "How did you get here so fast?"

"On my bicycle, sir."

Dad hired him on the spot to start work the next day. George Beers, another young fellow, was hired for the same kind of work. Both boys delivered radios to customers in a Model A Ford. Les Peppin stayed on at CFCY for ten years and learned a lot about the radio business, eventually being on the air most of the time announcing and operating. During the war he served as a wireless operator in lonely lighthouses keeping watch on submarines.

When Les was hired, Dad had one full time employee, Ian Cochrane. Ian was a tall, lanky youth whose looks resembled those of Charles Lindburg, the famous aviator; so, everyone called him "Lindy". Poor Lindy, though clever and sensitive, had all the awkwardness of gangling adolescence. He had started about six months earlier than Les, and had helped Tony Shelfoon build the new 100-watt transmitter.

Tony and Ian squabbled a lot, but they were both doing a good job of building the transmitter. Ian's forte was wiring, while Tony's was figuring out the intricacies of circuits. Dad was fond of them and amused by them both, so he smoothed over the ruffled feathers and kept them at it.

Towards the end of 1929, when the new Charlottetown Hotel was nearing completion, a small dynamo of a man by the name of John Quincy Adams breezed into the station, threw his hat on the office hat-rack and declared he was going to stay. He had been working on the electrical installation of the new hotel, and now that his work there was finished, he wanted to get a new job. From the start he called Dad, "Poppa." Jack Adams was short and wiry with skin the colour of parchment suggesting a long association with city life. He had the dapper appearance of the former New Yorker that he was. Jack nonchalantly claimed that he was descended from, not one, but two United States presidents. The cold bothered him, so in the winter he wore an old racoon coat, a left over from his college days. His hat, which he seemed to balance on top of his head, never reached his ears. In spite of his slight build and sallow complexion, John Quincy had tremendous drive and enthusiasm. Dad liked him and was impressed with his knowledge of the latest technology in electronics. He had big ideas about making a powerful radio station.

"You're operating on too low a power, Poppa" Jack would say.

Dad, of course, could not agree more.

"Get me some of the latest gear and we'll put in a water-cooled tube. Come on, Poppa, let's go for the 500 watts!"

Dad at this time was in the throes of a competitive battle for dominance with Jim Gesner and CHCK on the local scene. Also, Summerside's CHGS, the only other station on P.E.I., was seeking to move from 25 watts to 100 watts. He was aware that other broadcasters throughout the country were planning and preparing for a possible national network. Presently, he was operating at twice the output of CHCK, but it might be only a matter of time before they could equal his power. Dad was in the fray to win; so, he decided that in addition to be being the senior station he would be the most powerful. He and John Quincy started to put the plans into operation.

The water-cooled tube was ordered. It cost $400. This was the depression, and $400 was a fortune. But that was the least of the costs. The Department of Marine would not allow a station with its transmitter inside the city limits to operate on more than 250 watts. If CFCY wished to operate on 500 watts, it had to install a transmitter in a building of its own outside the city limits. Dad protested, but he quickly realized that if he was to maintain the dominant position, the power would eventually have to be increased. In addition to the transmitter building itself, he would require higher towers. For the time being he decided to operate on 250 watts which was still five times stronger than CHCK. He could move outside the city at a later date.

The arrival of the water-cooled tube produced great excitement, but its installation was disastrous. Lindy had been sent upstairs to the attic to sort through and test dozens and dozens of the small radio tubes that had accumulated over time. Any with life in them had to be salvaged, and catalogued. I was a teenager at the time, and Lindy's ruffled golden hair and slow drawl meant romance with a capital "R" to me. I had called in to see the new equipment. Jack Adams, who could produce the most colourful language, was deeply immersed in soldering wires. Dad was busy with plumbers who were installing at least thirty feet of pipe to carry the constant supply of water which flowed over the tube to maintain a steady temperature. I stood around hoping Dad would tell me to go and help Lindy with the tube sorting. But no one took any notice of me. So, bored with waiting around, I went off to the movies.

On the way home I called in to see how things were progressing. What a scene it was! Water was flowing everywhere. Jack was swearing a blue haze. Dad was trying to stem the tide of water with old coats, work clothes or anything else that came to hand, while cursing the day he'd ever heard of water-cooled tubes. During all this the man upstairs, Lindy, had been forgotten. As I stood there in disbelief at what I was seeing, Lindy descended the stairs carrying a large box filled with good tubes. Suddenly one big foot crossed over the other, and Lucky Lindy's luck gave out. Down he came with a tremendous crash, the hundred odd good tubes popping and splintering into a million glass fragments.

I got out of there as those tubes were bouncing down the steps and breaking into the growing pools of water made when "the baby wonder of the tube world"—as John Quincy called it—blew out. Poor Dad, I will never forget his face. Four hundred dollars plus whatever the broken tubes cost, not to mention the water damage—all in one afternoon. My father was in trouble. I cried all the way home.

When all the water was mopped up, all the tiny pieces of glass taken out of the floor boards, and when tempers had cooled to normal, it was discovered that the big water-cooled tubes were still intact, the splintering glass had only come from the small tubes that fell from Lindy's hands. The big ones were carefully placed in their heavily padded wooden containers and sent back to the factory to be rebuilt.

Chapter Ten

Art McDonald
Coins
"The Friendly Voice"

One of the first announcing jobs Les Peppin had was to announce the stock market. Nobody else liked to do it, and besides Les knew something about it. Les's father was involved in buying stocks and he and Les used to go and watch the board at the stockbroker's next door to the studio. On the day of the crash, Les saw that the market was edgy; it had been going up and down erratically all day. While he was on the air, all stocks dropped suddenly. The market went into a tailspin until it hit rock bottom, and millions of people went into shock.

I try to remember what the depression years were like and how our family was affected. I know the dreadful events which happened then with heads of large corporations jumping out of windows, armies of unemployed men riding freight trains from one end of the country to the other looking for work, the soup kitchens and the chronic despair— all these were things that were happening somewhere else. The Island with its compact family farms, and its deep cultural sense of community tended to provide a buffer against the more debilitating effects of the depression experienced elsewhere.

Living so far from the centre of things provided its own form of protection; because we were so used to it, people grouped together to help one another. The Island reverted back to a more primitive form of economics—the barter system. Dad called it "horse trading." Half a load of turnips was accepted for parts of a radio set; potatoes were given in exchange for announcements on the radio. Our world was one of make over and make do, inexpensive cuts of meat, lots of porridge, rice, and that all time favourite, tapioca, or "fisheyes" as my brother Bill called it. On our verandah there were cases of an insipid strawberry pop. The day it arrived from the bottler, my grandfather Smith was visiting. He appraised the stack of cases, then said dryly, "Did you buy that Keith, or did you talk for it?"

Dad worried that things would get so bad that we would not be able to get fresh milk; so he horse-traded for a cow one winter. Like many of the older houses then, ours had a barn at the back. What a hassle that cow turned out to be. She was always kicking over the pail and getting sick. One day she sprained her leg. Poor Dad knew very little about cows; but to him a sprain was a sprain, and he knew that Antiphlogistine poultices were good for sprains, inflammation, and just about everything else. So the cow got Antiphlogistine poultices. It was a horrible smelling goo that came in a lavender can that you submerged in a pot of boiling water until the goo was soft enough to spread and hot enough to blister the hide of an elephant. The poor cow kicked even harder then. Finally she got her dearest wish and was sent back to her former home on the farm. But still my memory of that cow is not the cloverish smell of fresh cream, but that of Antiphlogistine.

In those dismal days the radio played an important part in keeping people's minds off their worries, and as they tended to stay at home more, a radio set became an everyday necessity. The sales of radios, tubes, and batteries, though not large, enabled my Dad to stay in the business.

In order to try to raise a bit of extra cash, he diversified, and many strange things were sold from the front of the radio store. One dealership was an automatic card-dealing table for bridge players. It was such an innovation I doubt it would have caught on in the area even in good times. Although it didn't sell, it provided an endless source of fascination for my brother Bill. Oh yes, and there was the refrigerator—an early Norge with a large and cumbersome cooling system on top, half of which had to be dipped in hot water, and when that cooled, the procedure had to be started all over again. I remember the demonstration model sitting in our kitchen rumbling and shaking away like a sulking giant. These "get rich quick" schemes were desperate attempts to shore up the retail radio business, and every bit helped to keep the station on the air.

They say that disastrous things come in circumstances of three's. I really don't know if that is true or not, but for our family the Victoria Hotel Fire seemed to be a prelude to a series of reversals. In addition to the stock market crash and the onset of the Great Depression, the bottom fell out of the Prince Edward Island fox industry, and many of Grandfather WK's business interests plummeted.

Our house on Bayfield Street, which Dad believed was his, bought and paid for by "WK", was still in "WK's" name. The bank held a mortgage on it, and the upshot was we had to leave the home we loved and grew up in. Dad was heartbroken for his father, and "WK" was shocked at the suddenness of his reversals. It was really a dreadful and distressing time.

Saddened, we moved in with mother's father, Grandfather Smith. The crunch had come for "WK" as it had for so many. "WK", that most flamboyant of figures who drove around Charlottetown in large luxurious cars, who had made many business trips to Paris, London, and New York, and who had employed a full time Austrian, liveried chauffeur, was called into the bank to turn over his fox ranches forthwith. Characteristically, he waited until it was almost feeding time for the foxes. Then taking the huge bunch of keys to the pens, he marched into the bank manager's office and said:

"There are five hundred hungry foxes out there. Five o'clock is feeding time—you feed them!"

And with that he dropped the huge bunch of the keys with a clatter unto the desk and strolled out leaving an astounded bank manager to stare first at the keys and then at the stiff back and erect head leaving his office.

Tony Shelfoon said that CFCY's maturation was "...a long process of imperceptible progress; then suddenly it blossomed. Dad broke the ground, tended, weeded, nurtured until finally the bloom was safe. In plain words, to make a success of something one must have the right mix of vision, practicality, concentration, and courage to take risks."

One of my father's strengths was his ability to pick the right person for the job at the right time. Tony Shelfoon was exactly right to assist Dad through that very experimental stage; Les Peppin was right for the next ten years while he learned the "...radio business from the bottom up"; so was John Quincy Adams who built another more powerful transmitter. I single these three out because their contribution seemed to be

81

in direct proportion to their particular needs when they came to the station. It seems to have been that way with most people over the years who made a substantial contribution to CFCY. They came to the station when it was right for both of them at that particular time in their developments. Perhaps one of the most opportune of all hirings at CFCY was that of Louis Arthur McDonald, or as he liked to be known professionally, L.A. "Art" McDonald.

By 1935 the station was launched. The experimental stage was fairly well over; the worst of the depression had been weathered, and CFCY had originated programs to the Canadian Broadcasting Commission Network. The station at this time was at a critical stage. It needed someone to run it and to take care of the mountain of details that was becoming a part of its day to day operation.

"WK's" losses in the fox industry and his subsequent struggles with banks and creditors had taught Dad that sound accounting systems were essential. He was now dealing with national sponsors through ad agencies. Their demands for timing and spots were very exact. Local accounts also had to be sold, planned and programmed. The day was fast arriving when the drop-in atmosphere of the studio would have to change. Its growth would mean more staff which meant there would have to be standards and training, and, of course, a boss. Dad wanted to be free from all this. He wanted to be in a position to plan future directions and policies.

My father had hired Art McDonald in 1935. He had been at the station five years before and had returned to the type of work he loved most—broadcasting. He returned at a very busy period when the transmitter was being moved out to West Royalty. And even with all that activity, my father knew that he would have to move from Great George Street to an even bigger place. It was becoming apparent, also, that my father's attention would have to be focused more and more on working with other private broadcasters in the Maritimes and the rest of Canada to insure that the private station owners would receive fair treatment for their pioneering efforts. There were never-ending Parliamentary hearings into the future of broadcasting—on whether or not there should be full nationalization of the industry like the British BBC. At home here, in Canada, there was a full blown struggle looming between the private enterprisers and those in favour of outright nationalization.

Art in many ways was Dad's opposite number as far as temperament and personality were concerned. Both men were of quick intelligence, but Dad's was more introspective and undemonstrative. Art was quicksilver and volatile. When he applied for the job, he had just returned home from Boston where he had been working for the Edison Company, first as an accountant and then as an announcer. Prior to that he had been with the Bank of Nova Scotia, eventually achieving the rank of Assistant Accountant. Since his return from Boston, he had been working as Office Manager for the J.J. Hughes Company, Ltd., of Souris, Art's home town.

Anyone who knew Art would realize that working as a full time accountant would be a killer for him. He was too flamboyant, too creatively restless. An office job would have to be part of a larger and more stimulating package. Within that context, an office management job performed by Art would be meticulously accomplished. For example, when Keith Morrow—a few years later actually than the period I am describing now—was waiting for an interview in the outer office of the Brace Block, he nonchalantly sat back and put his feet up on the desk. Art came through, saw him, and fixed him with a penetrating stare from his piercing blue eyes, and roared at him, "Who do you think you are? Get those feet off that desk at once—this is a place of business!"

Art was thirty-seven when Dad interviewed him. They were both super-salesmen. Dad realized that Art was in many ways a tormented soul, an unfulfilled talent looking desperately for a chance. Art had a university education, having attended St. Dunstan's in Charlottetown; this, plus his business and broadcasting experience added to his daring and energy was exactly what Dad needed to make things work. Art was a maverick who could pull things off and pull others into line if he had to.

"I'm looking for a man who will build this station up. Who will organize the staff, the office, and the programs. In fact, if he proves himself, will be Director and next in rank to me," Dad said to Art.
"I'd like to try that, Colonel." Art answered.
"Okay. Come in as soon as you are ready."

Art, in addition to the other qualities I have mentioned, was an Islander through and through. He loved Souris and was proud of his roots there. He knew what Prince Edward Islanders liked and he set about tailoring the programming to suit them. One of Art's first moves was to bring in a young singing cowboy called "Tex" Cochrane, the Yodelling Trail Rider. Les Peppin was sent down to the Borden train to meet him. What a sensation he created with his magnificent black cowboy hat, his buffalo chaps, his low-slung belt, and his boots and spurs that jingle-jangled when he walked. "Tex" was tall and lean, and when he strolled along the streets of Charlottetown, guitar slung over his shoulder, people turned to stare, and children skipped along the street behind him.

Gordon, "Tex" Cochrane, a handsome, wholesome boy who hailed from Sweet's Corner, near Windsor, Nova Scotia had his heart set on having a successful career as a radio and a recording singing star. He admired Wilf Carter who had a triple-type yodel, but it was a long time before he could master the technique. Tex wrote his own songs and put this difficult yodel into "Echo Yodel Lullaby" and it was his most popular recording for RCA Victor. Out of forty original songs, sixteen were recorded.

I remember that Tex Cochrane joined George Chappelle and "The Merry Islanders", a six-piece band that played at concerts, followed by dances in community centres. All of their concerts were completely sold out. As well as these barn-storming tours around the Island, they played regularly on the coast-to-coast network of the CBC from CFCY. Later, Tex toured with Don Messer for a year, but when war broke out he became one of the most enthusiastic members of Dad's signaller's unit and from that training he decided to serve his country and join up. He went overseas with the North Nova Scotia Highlanders in 1943 and was part of the liberation of Holland. Typically he doesn't talk about the action, but he said that he and Mike McTague bought a guitar in Holland and they used to sing during lulls in the fighting. When the war was over Tex made a career in the army and retired a Major in 1963. I remember him always as a modest person, never really believing that he was good enough to become a top western singer, but lately, 46 years after he recorded his own songs, they have been re-recorded by a German company and he is getting fan letters from far away places, even East Germany. The songs he wrote always stressed family ties and I heard some of them not long ago on a CBC program. Art Mcdonald, an excellent promoter of talent, was solidly behind Tex.

Art made great changes at CFCY almost overnight. It was he who gave the station its slogan, "The Friendly Voice of the Maritimes."

Indeed he **was** the friendly voice. He was a superb performer with an intimate, easy-to-listen to voice. The public image he projected was one of warmth, sincerity, and humanity. Art loved his radio audience in the way a great actor loves his audience, and he projected this through the microphone. The private man was restless and complex. There was a tragic history of tuberculosis in his family. Art, himself, was a sufferer, and typical of those who are, he was prone to fits of depression and irritability. After he was at CFCY for about a year he and Dad did not see eye to eye over a certain matter, so he left for a while. But he and CFCY needed each other, and it was not too long before there were compromises and understandings, and L.A "Art" McDonald was back on the job again, more energetic than ever.

In 1936 he wrote, compiled and edited a CFCY magazine called The Friendly Voice. It was no run-off-on-the duplicator affair, but a beautifully laid out two-colour print job with pictures on good quality paper. As I look at it, I am amazed at how professional it was and the time it must have taken him to put it together, but Art was indefatigable. He really was Mr. CFCY, even to the point of having had made a large black onyx ring emblazoned with the letters CFCY in gold with a pair of cuff-links to match. He was responsible for bringing Don Messer to the Island, and between the two of them they made CFCY a household word from coast to coast.

When the word came from Ottawa that he had to locate his new 500 watt transmitter outside of the city limits, Dad had to forage around for the things he needed but couldn't afford: two steel towers at least 100 hundred feet high each, brick, lumber, labour and many other requirements. True to his fashion, Dad did what he always did when he had worries and problems to solve — he went fishing. Away he'd go tramping along his favourite streams until late evening when he headed home again with a basket of trout. He got to work right away — horse trading. Over the next weeks loads of yellow brick arrived at the site from the L.E. Shaw brickworks, and lumber arrived from Paoli's lumber yard.

The towers, however, are a story onto themselves. Dad knew that the two steel towers used by the Canadian National Railways Radio Station, CNRA in Moncton, had been dismantled when the Canadian National went out of the radio business. Where were they? He turned on his amateur radio transmitter, VE1HI, and put the word out to all his friends that he was trying to locate the two 150 foot towers.

Eventually word came back to him that they had been dismantled into numbered sections and stored in a Government warehouse somewhere near Ottawa. These towers were not new, but they were all he could afford at the time. He quickly snapped them up at a warehouse price. They were shipped down to Prince Edward Island on a railroad flatcar. The delivery from the rail siding must have been spectacular, for there were only clay roads then. The site in those days was in the country, but today it is the location for a large shopping mall. How they got the tons of steel delivered there, whether by teams of horses or tractors, or both, I'll never know; but I do know their arrival and subsequent erection was the talk of the Island, and Dad was whispered about being that nut Rogers again.

To erect steel towers of that weight and height requires the professional skills of trained journeymen. Luckily, the Island hockey team, the Abbies, had two players who had been enticed to come down from Quebec and Ontario to play in the "Big Four" hockey league; Ray Stull and Harry Richardson, the players, were also experienced steel erectors. They stayed over after the hockey season and sorted out and erected the towers between them. The building of the transmitter house was supervised by George Morrison, a master carpenter who worked with Dad. On the day the towers were nearing completion, Dad called my mother on the phone:

"Flo, the steel is rising, I wanted you to know."

That's all he could say. He was overcome with emotion. My mother told me he was weeping, but his tears were tears of joy. How far he had come in radio with these giants of steel since the day he had erected his father's ladder to sling a crude aerial from chimney to barn.

Chapter Eleven

Radio Landmark
at
Moose River

O ver the next few months the response to the increased power and the towers was overwhelming. Letters poured in by the bagsful from all over the Maritime provinces and from remote Newfoundland and Labrador outports, not to mention the entire northeastern part of Quebec. The number of national and local sponsors more than doubled. Even the newspapers lauded the strength and clarity of the signal. The well known New Brunswick editor, C.C. Avard of the Sackville Tribune wrote:

...I have long felt that station CFCY has dominated the Maritime field as far as radio is concerned...The supremacy of CFCY...has been accomplished through long years of well directed effort...(as a result of) toil upward into the night as well as into the day...I know at least two reasons why CFCY rules the Martime roost and they are two steel towers 150 high as well as 600 watts soon to be 1000 watts; mechanical facilities of notable excellence...and capable management of Keith Rogers is a credit to Prince Edward Island...You and I have a lot in common, Keith, old boy, but not the radio, of course, as newspapers are supposed to be the deadly enemies of broadcasting stations.

It was also very gratifying to Dad that two of the most prominent Maritime newspapers, The Halifax Herald and The Halifax Mail signed a long term contract as co-sponsors of CFCY's popular program "The Outports". This was an indication that perhaps the dust was settling between some of the newspaper editors and broadcasters.

Dad started "The Outports" program in 1933 to fill in an off-hour in radio—five to six in the evening. The early theme called "Memories" describes the program exactly:

"Memories, Memories,
Tales of long ago..."

The old songs of the British Isles were played with a sprinking of comic songs. Everything from cowboy music to the bagpipes, whatever was requested. Moore & McLeod, one of Charlottetown's leading department stores and the first sponsor of "The Outports" program received thousands of letters containing requests. The farmers loved it so much they put back milking time an hour earlier. Typical of the many fan letters that came in to this program is the following: "We milk an hour earlier and make five to six our supper and rest hour to enjoy the old-time favourite songs." Eventually Art McDonald took over "The Outports" more and more at that time until he became synonymous with it. Later Ray Simmons ran the program for a period of 22 years. The amount of fan mail was so great from Eastern Canada and New England, that the Halifax Herald had to issue special pleas to fans not to write any more letters until the girls in their office had attended to all those already received.

In 1931 Dad had incorporated and the Island Radio Company had become the Island Radio Broadcasting Company Ltd. In the process of doing this he gave John Quincy Adams a share and listed him as one of the incorporators. From that moment on, John Quincy regarded himself as the senior employee and a "member of the firm". When Art McDonald arrived on the scene it was hate at first sight.

They each held their separate titles—Art's was Station Manager and Program Director: John Quincy's was Chief Engineer. They squabbled over who had the most authority, John Quincy believing he had because he had been there longer and owned a share. If one of them wanted the other to do something, the other would think of a dozen reasons why he shouldn't. Sometimes their stubborn rivalry worked to the detriment of the station—like the time we moved studio and offices to the Brace Block on Queen Street and the transmitter out to the new plant at West Royalty.

Art had planned the move from Great George Street to a "T". He was determined not to lose one minute of air time. Dad had recently purchased a new Gage amplifier and had it delivered and installed in the awaiting new studio. We had a small portable console over which Les Peppin did announcements and played record after record while Art had the rest of the equipment delivered and set up piecemeal.

The plan was to move the console immediately after the station signed off the air at midnight. All during this the fur flew between John Quincy and Art, but Art got his way until it came time to move the transmitter out to its new building at West Royalty. When that time came, the "Chief Engineer" hotly maintained he **could** and **would** handle the transmitter transference without a hitch.

"It is my responsibility as Chief Engineer, Art," he proclaimed, "so you keep you nose out of it and make sure the programs are on schedule."

"But if you foul it up, Jack, I won't be able to keep to any schedule, and that's what's worrying me. I don't want one second of air time lost on this station," Art needled back.

"Damit, McDonald, you just watch me!"

With that John Quincy grabbed a pair of pliers and with great ostentation, he randomly snipped transmitter wires left, right, and centre. His burst of bad temper over, it took him hours to figure which wire belonged to which; and as a result, CFCY was off the air for three full days.

Art was furious, with perhaps just a bit of perverse delight at the same time. But I do not wish to give the impression that Jack Adams was an incompetent dunderhead, or that this is how Art saw him. Even though Art was mad at him most of the time, he had a grudging respect for his technical ability, and when credit was due, he gave it, like the time during the Moose River Mine Disaster. Here is what Art wrote about John Quincy Adams' work:

...the grim and yet heroic story of the Moose River Gold mine involved long hours of continuous transmission...one single continuous run lasting twenty-one and a half hours, another eighteen hours...in order to do this our transmitter and all apparatus involved must needs be functioning perfectly, and our thanks are due to our good Chief Engineer, Mr. John Q. Adams whose long shifts necessitated his bearing the brunt of much of the announcing as well. To Announcer Les Peppin too, we pass a bouquet...

The Moose River Gold Mine Disaster that Art McDonald wrote about began on April 12, 1936. Dr. D.E. Robertson, a noted Ontario medical doctor and H.B. Magill, a thirty-five year old lawyer also from Ontario, were inspecting a gold mine they owned in Moose River, Nova Scotia. Guided by their timekeeper, Alfred Scadding, they had worked their way down to the 350 foot level. At this point, they heard the dreaded rumble of subsidence. The earth caved in on them, and thousands of tons of rock and clay blocked their way out.

It was not known at first whether the three men were alive, but rescue operations were begun at once. Eleven Stellarton, Nova Scotia draegermen dug and burrowed their way through the blocked underground channels foot by painful foot without a trace or hint of the buried men. Discouraged, they were just about to quit when a thin whiff of smoke was detected wafting through a crevice. It was interpreted as a signal from the trapped men. **They were alive**.

Rescue efforts were vigourously begun anew. The Stellarton men were joined by miners from Cape Breton and by hard rock miners from Ontario. A special diamond drill brought in for the occasion bored a two inch hole through solid rock, through which food and medical supplies were lowered to the trapped men. The rescue team, now forty men, worked around the clock, and there was great hope that the three men would be brought out alive. But due to exposure to the damp and cold, Magill developed pneumonia and died eight days after the rescue work began. The men worked furiously on, because added to Magill's death were new threats of cave-ins. In two days time they were only twelve feet away from the remaining two survivors and their dead comrade. Release was expected hourly.

When word that the men might be alive reached the Canadian Radio Broadcasting Commission's newsroom in Halifax, J. Frank Willis grabbed a desk microphone and whatever meagre equipment he could lay his hands on, and with his colleagues from CHNS, Arleigh Canning and Cecil Landry, rushed to the disaster site where they began a round-the-clock narration of the rescue operations.

Willis' dramatic voice and vivid narration transfixed listeners in front of their radio sets across the whole of North America. They felt they were actually standing there at the pit head. Throughout the ten days of the operation, work stopped, people cried and held prayer vigils in the fervent hope that the exhausted rescue workers would be successful.

The Moose River Broadcasts, as they came to be called, were the first significant actuality radio news reports in North America. It was a marathon with radio stations on the air night and day. All of the 58 radio stations in Canada carried the broadcasts and 650 radio stations in the United States of the Mutual, Columbia and National broadcasting networks did so as well, broadcasting reports every hour on the hour. Dad never closed down radio station CFCY as long as the reports were coming in, and during the final days we stayed on the air all night long. The lone voice of Frank Willis, brimming with emotion and compassion, was the focal point for millions of people as they heard his account of the last stages of the rescue:

The men are coming out. The rescue has been accomplished. This long looked for victory is now in our hands, and those men are coming out! And I tell you ladies and gentlemen—words almost fail me to describe this macabre, this grotesque scene at the head of this pit—it's like something from the Arabian Nights. I'll remember it to the last of my life. It is the most spectacular thing I have ever witnessed. Those few lights glimmering down on the hundreds of miners from all over Canada, waiting there, watching to see their victory finally accomplished.

The relief felt was in proportion to the intensity shared, and the pealing of church bells could be heard throughout the land.

There were equally close ties between CFCY and the listeners in

91

Nova Scotia and New Brunswick. Before the establishment of local broadcasting stations in northern Nova Scotia, CFCY was treated as the local station in that area. Where now Antigonish, New Glasgow, Truro and Amherst have their own stations, CFCY was the only one and it enjoyed a large, loyal audience built up over many years. A wide variety of sporting and special events were broadcast from time to time and as well, CFCY was able to provide a service to many businesses in the counties of Antigonish, Pictou, Colchester and Cumberland through radio advertising of their goods and services. Many valued relationships, both business and with individual listeners, were formed over a period of well over a quarter of a century.

Perhaps one of the people from eastern Nova Scotia we saw most frequently was J. "Hy" Goodman. He was in charge of the advertising and publicity for the largest department store in the area and he would come over to "voice" his own commercials, recording on large aluminum discs enough to last a week. He would sail on the S.S. Hochelaga from Pictou around Point Prim and into Charlottetown harbour. The boat would only take about four cars and the crossing would be four hours long. Later on he would fly with Carl Burke on his seven-passenger "butterfly" plane from Trenton to Charlottetown. This would take about twenty minutes and the cost was $7 one way. He told me that he remembers both modes of travel as usually being very rough. "Hy" was listening the night in 1923 that Jack Dempsey was defending his heavyweight championship against "Wild Bill Firpo".

"I had only one earphone and by then a little one-tube set. Your father was re-broadcasting from an American station, picking it up on a powerful receiving set he had built. It was coming in fine, but once in a while the broadcast would fade out and Keith Rogers, with only a bare knowledge of the fight world, would take up earphones connected to the set and try to re-create the atmosphere of the ring for us. When the signal strengthened, he would give a deep sigh of relief and leave the rest of the broadcast to the experts."

Art McDonald persuaded my father in 1937 that it was time to open a studio in New Glasgow and in collaboration with The Goodman

Company a room adjacent to their large new auditorium was chosen. It was made sound-proof and had a large window of triple glass.

The first tentative efforts from there were the programs of recorded music and it was an important event when Art McDonald went over to describe first hand, the Inaugural Ball on January 27, 1937.

The New Glasgow Evening News wrote:

"The new auditorium is thought to be the finest in the Maritimes with six thousand square feet of glistening, gleaming unobstructed floor space."

The Gyro Club had whipped up enthusiasm for months and the Ball, by invitation only, was considered to be the most colourful social event of the decade. The place that night was packed, all the ladies in beautiful floor-length gowns and the men in tuxedos. Waldo Goodman, Hy's brother, described the scene to me:

"It was an invited party in a brand new hall with a ten-piece band, "The Peerless Orchestra". CFCY was doing the first "live" broadcast from the new auditorium and the Mayor and other dignitaries were scheduled to speak over the station during the evening. It was thought that the plans had been made right down to the last detail. However, the parking lot had not been paved and apparently cinders came in on people's feet. The varnish on the floor had only been completed the day before and it hadn't hardened properly. About the fourth dance we looked at the floor which had just been waxed and it was starting to roll off like snow. The edges of the ladies gowns were all dirty... all of the shoes were blackened. It was a real mess, but strangely enough no one left. They had come to have a good time, and they were going to have one! We had to stop the dancing and clean the whole floor with brooms and mops. And the dance then continued until the early hours of the morning."

Art, never at a loss for words, threw away his notes and gave an impromptu description of events.

In 1937 also, we began broadcasting sixteen hours a day, from eight in the morning until midnight. The increasing expense and the longer hours of programming drove my father to search for additional revenues to meet these new expenses and he began to hire additional announcers and technicians.

CFCY had a warm and happy association with business firms all along the northern part of Nova Scotia...Neima, Margolian, McCullouch and Sobey, to name just a few, along with the Roseland Theatre in New Glasgow and the Jubilee in Stellarton all became friends of the Station and we, in turn, did many hours of broadcasting for them. We began to have applications for jobs from the area and through the years many Nova Scotians worked at the station: Whit Carter, Sandy Hoyt, Bill Graham, Merrill Young, Max Corkum, Ed Watters, Dorothy MacDonald, Henry Purdy, Borden MacDonald, John Fanjoy, Ted Hale and Coralee Pugh and many others. Dozens of talented people came over to broadcast and I remember one special night when we had almost all of the Pictou Highland Pipe Band in our studio along with their pipes and drums.

The listeners there and in other parts of the Martimes were prolific letter writers. If they liked a program they were appreciative and if they didn't like what we were doing, we would hear about it. The sports fans, hockey, baseball, horse racing fans sent a torrent of letters our way. Listeners also asked for plenty of the old Irish and Scotch music and old time fiddling.

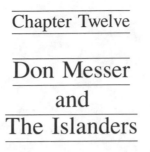

Chapter Twelve

Don Messer
and
The Islanders

Since the early 1930's there is evidence that the Canadian Radio broadcasting Commission (as the CBC was known then) realized the scope of traditional music on Prince Edward Island. Traditional music in the twenties was flourishing on the Island and CFCY was largely responsible for keeping it alive. The old-time fiddlers like Jay and Weeks used to broadcast from our home. The Outports program was mainly old time music, and of course, Chappelle's "Merry Islanders", Colin Boyd, Jack Webster, Al Dowling, Alyre Gallant and a host of others kept traditional music vital.

In 1926 a mammoth fiddling competition was held at the Strand Theatre in Charlottetown. The first prize was a paid trip to Boston to represent the Island in an international competition. Play-offs were held from one end of the Island to the other, culminating in the finals in Charlottetown on March 30. Special train excursions brought crowds in for the event. Snowfall was so heavy that tunnels had to be dug across main streets, and a big crowd from Souris was snowbound on the train for several days, prolonging the finals. The theatre was packed to bursting as over 1,200 people crowded into it to hear Neil Cheverie from Souris win first prize. CFCY carried the entire show, thrilling thousands all over the snowbound Island, and James M. Cameron, Nova Scotian historian recalls that when he was about twelve he heard this broadcast. He was standing outside the music store in New Glasgow, Nova Scotia on a Saturday shopping night. Traffic on the main street couldn't move because of the crowd in front of the loud speaker. When a fiddler would

Courtesy of Margaret Chappelle MacLean

The Merry Islanders, 1937-1938.

Courtesy of Cleaveland & Ruby MacLean

Lt. to Rt. Waldo Munro, Ray Simmons, Marg Osburne, Cecil McEachern, Warren MacRae, Julius "Duke" Nielsen, Don Messer, Charlie Chamberlain.

stop, the crowd in the street would applaud. So keen was the interest in fiddling that it even provoked sermons against it from a few pulpits.

Later an old-time orchestra was formed under the direction of Bob Weeks—he had won third place in the 1926 competition—and broadcast to the Radio Commission's Maritime network on at least two occasions in 1934. George Chappelle's "Merry Islanders" went coast-to-coast on network programs in the winter of 1937. The tradition of maintaining old-time music on CFCY culminated in the signing on of Don Messer and his Islanders as resident professionals in very early 1940.

One of CFCY's first and most active sponsors was Kelly and McInnis, a popular men's clothing store. Art McDonald had sold the account, but the store owners had most of the say as to what, or who was to go on the air. Mr. McInnis himself was fond of dropping into the studio to say a few words to the customers about any bargains or specials he was putting on. Like most of the broadcasting from Great George street, everything in the beginning was casual and unplanned.

I know of one person who later became well known to all Maritime radio listeners, who started out by winning the Kelly & McInnis Talent Contest. Ches Cooper sang the old Wilf Carter song, "I'm Going to Ride to Heaven on a Stream-lined Train" and won the first prize of a suit of clothes. It was worth $22.00 then and it represented almost a month's pay when Ches was teaching school in a rural area.

Ches told me that returning to the little village where he lived after the broadcast was a special thrill for him.

"Radio in those days was the same as going to Hollywood, almost. The first time I sang on the radio and drove back home, I went down to Prowse's store, the local store in Murray Harbor and all of the people said, 'I heard you on the radio today', and I was just like a celebrity from Hollywood."

Years later, Ches originated a program devoted to agriculture on CFCY and after appearing on both radio and television on Prince Edward Island over a period of twelve years became a well-known agricultural commentator for the CBC in Halifax, host of Country Calendar and on Radio Noon. Ches always says that CFCY was like a family and

97

*Ches Cooper and Loman McAulay were
popular with the listeners on their early
morning show.*

I agree with him, but I am inclined to think of it too as a friendly sort
of club in the early days.

Later when the station moved to the Brace Block on Queen Street,
Art McDonald with his usual flair and energy, organized an Island wide
talent contest.

Art, to use a modern expression, hyped it up over the air, and soon
the contest was considered to be a very big thing indeed. Talent poured
in from one end of the Island to the other. There were no formal
auditions. Art simply got a prospective competitor aside, listened to
a few bars of their playing or singing, and if he liked them told them
they were on. The rules were simple. Once all the competitors were
in the studio, they were not allowed out until the program was over.
The winner was decided by the most number of votes from the listening
public.

Raymond Selleck, who sang and yodelled "My Swiss Sweetheart

Lullaby" while his sister, Fanny Bertram, accompanied him on the piano, almost tied for first place with a man from Cardigan who played the guitar and mouth organ at the same time. Art told Raymond he would have won had he gone out and canvassed a few more votes. Apparently there was so much enthusiasm generated by the contest that family and community members got actively involved stirring up votes. These contests became a weekly feature for a while until Kelly and McInnis replaced them with a regular program. Ray Selleck's and his sister's performance got them invited back to sing with violinist Percy Groom. Also in the group, was Fanny's husband, Fred Bertram who played the harmonica, and Stirling and Syd Stead, Oliver Ross and Frank Johnson.

It was out of these early talent competitions and subsequent programs that CFCY's tradition of country music developed. Prior to the arrival of Don Messer, there was a group called "The Merry Makers" started by George Chappelle with Walter Ferguson and Leo Molyneaux in 1935. They played the old traditional Irish, French and Scottish tunes for lancers and square dancing passed down to them from an older generation. Many guests appeared on the program, one being a twelve year old, Heber MacAusland, "the Yodelling Islander". A year later, George formed a larger five-man band and they were re-named "The Merry Islanders". Their theme, "Up the River" set toes tapping. The program was so popular it ran for about ten years throughout the winter months.

Early in this period, Julius "Duke" Nielsen, who became Don Messer's bass player and of whom it was said, Arthur Fiedler invited to join the Boston Pops Orchestra, would play periodically with the Merry Islanders. Ray Selleck who became Merry Islanders principal vocalist and guitarist recalls:

We'd just get started over the air putting on the program and we'd see Duke looking in through the little window. And the first thing he'd sneak in, get a bass, and he'd stand there and play with us.

When we moved to the Brace Block, the public got used to being inside the studio, because so many of them had come through to participate in the talent competitions, and because so many of them had been used to dropping in to entertain and be entertained when we were on Great George Street. The visitors used to annoy Art who wanted to make the studio more formal and professional, but he'd get the chairs, anyway, and line them around the wall. The performers liked the live audience there and felt as if they were playing directly to and for them rather than to the critical operators looking back at them through the plate glass window of the control room.

Art McDonald was an inveterate showman, and even though he disapproved of the studio audience he couldn't help putting on a show for them. Before the broadcast would begin, he would very ceremoniously produce a roll of bright red ribbon and meticulously measure distances between the mikes. Then he would position himself before each mike in turn, and with great concentration hold an end of the ribbon between his teeth and hold an arm's length distance of ribbon to the mike. In this way he presumably was setting up the correct speaking distance. The exercise was, in fact, meaningless, but everyone was impressed as they watched, in silence, Art carry out this ritual. It was taken as a sign of great professionalism.

When "The Merry Islanders" hit the air to the tune of "Up The River" it was fun and everybody joined in. Bill Brown, who was an announcer then, would get up in the middle of a fast number and do a step dance, and Bob Large who was an operator on his way to the control booth would let out a lusty "Yahooo." Some of the Merry Islanders were farmers like Ray Sellick and the Bertrams. It is a testimony to how much they enjoyed performing that they would make it into town every Friday night through many a wild Island snowstorm— and most likely on horse and sled too.

Ray Simmons, who later played with Don Messer, was a member of "The Merry Islanders" for about a year and travelled with them playing for dances in centres all over the Maritimes and the Gaspé during the summer.

"I always got along well with George Chappelle because he was a heck of a nice guy," says Ray. But Art McDonald who wasn't with us, had many arguments with George when the band was on the road. I didn't know Art McDonald from a hole in the ground, but I got a letter from him ordering me to paint all the signs of CFCY off the trailer we used for luggage and instruments". No one knows how the argument between George Chappelle and Art would have been resolved, because the war broke out and many of the boys joined up.

100

Art was responsible for bringing Don Messer to CFCY from New Brunswick as Musical Director and orchestra leader in 1939. Don brought Charlie Chamberlain with him. It was a very shrewd move indeed, because Art realized that throughout the network CFCY was becoming synonymous with traditional music, and it was identifiable with a typical "down east" flavour. Art figured that it was time to search for talent that would have national as well as regional appeal. He found it in Don Messer. Don was a perfectionist, a true professional, and an original. He placed his emphasis, not on his own image as a performer, but on what he performed—the mark of true humility in a true artist. His unassuming and shy manner made you think perhaps of a talented uncle or cousin playing at a party in the kitchen. Charlie Chamberlain, a natural singer, never knew how good he was. Charlie was brought up to hard physical labour from an early age, and even after he was quite well known he often washed and waxed cars to bring in a little extra, and he was as proud of his ability to do this as well as he was of singing.

Not long after the orchestra had arrived on the Island, a ground system was being installed at CFCY's transmitter site. Miles of wire had to be buried in the ground. Charlie Chamberlain heard about it and hired himself and his car out to do the job. At that time all the members of the band were scrambling for part-time work as the pay from the network and their share of dance receipts would not sustain them. Ray Simmons, Duke Nielsen and Charlie went out to bury the wire. Duke was very, very energetic and between them, they formulated what they thought was a brilliant plan. They would make a plough and bury the wire using Charley's old car. So they attached the plough to the back of the car. Charley took hold of the plough to make the furrow that the wire was to lie in. Duke took the wheel of the car. Off he went at much too high a speed dragging Charlie behind him, hollering and running to keep up but Duke never stopped. Well, the Duke didn't last too long. Charlie got mad and fired him from the job. Duke Nielson decided he'd use his after-rehearsal hours running projection machines in the theatres and Charlie and Ray finished the job at the transmitter. Charlie, like all good artists, performed his songs with a great deal of heart and love for his fellow man. He remained totally oblivious to his stardom until the end.

In New Brunswick Charlie and Don were known as "The Singing Lumberjacks". Later they were joined by Julius "Duke" Nielsen,

101

another brilliant musician who was the talented player of 16 different instruments. Duke's best instrument was the bass fiddle and that is what he payed most of the time. That and the banjo. Don, Duke and Charlie teamed up with Ned Landry, Eldon Rathburn, and Joe LeBlanc for "The Backwoods Breakdown". Later the group headed by Don, Charlie and Duke were known as "The New Brunswick Lumberjacks." Sometimes as many as fifteen musicians played with them and they broadcast on the Canadian Broadcasting Commission programs from CHSJ Saint John.

When they moved to Charlottetown, Jackie Doyle former pianist with George Chappelle, joined them and also Bill LeBlanc and the MacRae cousins, Harold and Warren on the drums and trumpet. Marg Osburne, "The Girl From The Singing Hills" came to Charlottetown to sing with Don Messer in 1947. Cecil McEachern joined the Islanders the same year as Marg and Waldo Munro was the popular pianist in the later years. They were all of them very accomplished musicians and rugged individualists; and it says something for their quiet little leader that he was able to keep them practicing long hours perfecting their style. Don Messer was involved in broadcasting for forty years.

Art McDonald did the announcing for the program on the coast-to-coast network in the early years. He was announcing on their first broadcast to the CBC network, Nov. 11th, 1939. He would come on the air with:

"From the studios of CFCY in Charlottetown, Prince Edward Island, it's the way down east music of Don Messer and his Islanders!"

Then Charlie would sing:

"Got my dancin' boots on
Got my Sunday best
Dancing to the Islanders tonight!"

and they'd be away on a program that reached at one time well over three million people. Later the announcing job was done by Bob Large when

Art took sick and by Ray Simmons for many years. Don Tremaine announced the program on television from Halifax. Ray was always a member of the band and did the Outports Program on CFCY, but perhaps he is best known as a clarinetist with Don and was loved and respected by his many fans.

Don knew what his audiences wanted to hear and on quick, recognizable and danceable tunes, he built his enormous popularity.

Folklorists Dorothy & Homar Hogan credit him with influencing other fiddlers with a style as clean, straight-ahead and neat as a well-tended farm and marked by "down-to-earth" simplicity.

The band had made 18 tours by 1969 and a Centennial trip for Festival Canada in 1967 lasted three months and covered sixty-one centres. More than thirty-five 78's were recorded by Apex, mostly compositions of Don Messer.

Composer at work. Don Messer, who once fiddled all night for 35 cents, wrote all the arrangements for his shows.

It isn't often that someone you see every day becomes famous but I felt that special warm feeling for Don when I read three large columns in the Encyclopedia of Music in Canada which describes "The Islanders", "The most popular old time music group in Canada during the mid-20th Century."

One of Don's fiddles was placed in the Country Music Hall of Fame in Nashville and his library and papers are in the Public Archives of Nova Scotia.

I believe the most moving tribute paid to Don Messer and the Islanders was by Maritime poet Alden Nowlan in Weekend Magazine in 1979. He wrote that his father was a real Don Messer fan:

"Having come home from the sawmill where he worked, stopping in the dooryard to shake the sawdust out of his overalls and shirt and to wash in cold water in a basin on the back steps, and having washed down his supper with countless cups of brick-colored tea, he would roll and light a cigarette (his third and last of the day) and then tune in to the Islanders. Out of the old battery-operated Marconi would come the guy-next-door voice of Ray Simmons, then Charlie Chamberlain would sing and Don and the boys would break into "The Operator's Reel" or "The Devil's Dream" and my father no matter how weary he must have been after 9 hours at work, would tap his toes in time to the music.

Men like my father cried when they heard in 1973 that Don Messer was dead. I doubt that any artist can be paid a higher tribute than that.

Chapter Thirteen

A Secret Visit
from
Princess Juliana

When Dad purchased CHCK from Jim Gesner and his Board of Directors in 1938, it was a difficult decision. He couldn't afford to buy it and on the other hand, he couldn't afford not to do so. He also had the problem of meeting the official regulations required of him to run two fully licenced stations. There was no feeling of joy at owning CHCK, but owning it meant that it was out of circulation. Charlottetown simply wasn't big enough to sustain two commercial radio stations. Had he closed CHCK down, that is, allowed the licence to run out, it would have afforded an opportunity for another competitor who wished to apply for it. He had fought a long and difficult battle with Gesner to gain control, and he was not about to let the broadcasting situation deteriorate to the cut-throat competition and animosity he had experienced.

Regulations demanded that CHCK be aired for several hours each day. By this time CFCY, now part of the national network, was blossoming and Dad was on the look out for good potential operators and announcers. Why not use CHCK to train them? It had very few listeners; so, for a few hours each day trainees could use it to stretch their vocal cords. Also it could be used to try out new ideas without disrupting the main programming of CFCY.

Syd Kennedy, Keith Morrow, John MacEwen, Ray Simmons, Ira Stewart and Loman McAulay among others, learned how to be broadcasters in the afternoons on CHCK. My brother Bill was then seventeen and had won many music competitions, the main one being his song and piano compositions in a Quebec Music Festival open to all of Canada. He had performed several classical programs on the CBC network and Dad thought he should try out as an announcer, so for a time, he and Ray Simmons split the afternoon programs on CHCK. When Bill left for New York to study at the Julliard School of Music, John MacEwen teamed up with Ray on CHCK. John and Ray say that they got their start as announcers in the little room at the top of the stairs over White's Restaurant. Later, John became Director of Radio for CBC based in Halifax and Ray Simmons became well known across Canada as clarinetist and announcer on the Don Messer Radio Show. John says that he and Ray were "fledglings" together.

Garnhum Photo

William Keith Rogers. Later Music Director at CFCY.

"If you could do a reasonably good job on CHCK, you were then allowed to try out on the larger station CFCY. One thing I remember most fondly was the amount of freedom that was given to individual announcers to choose their own material. We had Standard and Langworth Transcription Libraries and hundreds of commercial recordings. It was a fine library and I got to know it well as one of my first assignments was to catalogue hundreds of cards."

Bill Brown, who had been at CFCY almost four years doing news reporting and sports broadcasting, and Syd Kennedy started the "Early Birds". They wrote the skits and ran the program. Jack Adams, the Chief engineer and his assistant Bob Large would join in from the transmitter and Les Peppin from the control room. It was a breakfast club type of program and they were allowed the greatest latitude. Sometimes Syd would play beautiful music and read poetry. Listeners sent in material too, quite often under assumed names. One listener from Antigonish called herself "Rara Avis" meaning rare bird. No one knew who she was. Syd, who was outgoing and friendly with a tremendous sense of humour, used her letters regularly over a three year period and it became a "friendship through the air", neither having met the other. He read her funny stories and her poetry. Later when she was a member of the Wartime Prices and Trade Board, she went in to see him at his Halifax office at the CBC. Her name was Eileen Cameron Henry and she still lives in Antigonish N.S. where she was Deputy Mayor. Mrs. Henry has published in Ladies Home Journal and Chatelaine and has written three books of poetry, "Comfort Me with Apples", "Dancer In The Dust" and "An Ancient Sea".

"The Early Birds" developed a large audience among convalescents and on one occasion Syd, Bill and Les travelled to New Glasgow, Nova Scotia where their broadcast originated at the bedside of a shut-in listener, Mary Helen Brown who signed her inspirational letters, "Scraps".

One day, the Early Birds played the music for an actual wedding. One of their regular listeners was getting married and she lived in a remote district of Nova Scotia and would be married at home. They had no piano or musical instruments. "I would be ever so grateful to our favourite radio station, CFCY, if you would play the Wedding March for me on the air."

This of course excited the imagination of Syd Kennedy who was incurably romantic. He chose the right recording and wrote, assuring the bride-to-be that he would carry out her wishes at the precise time on the correct date. We were all listening and work came to a stand-still in the office. We could imagine the young bride at the head of the stairs, flowers in her hand, slowly descending...Listeners were told what was happening and it was an auspicious moment, the highlight of the broadcasting week. After it was over, Syd reached for his next recording and to our horror we heard the then popular song ring out...

"Boo Hoo..you've got me crying for you

Boo Hoo...you left me waiting at the church..."

That is as far as it went...Syd quickly grabbed the record off the turntable. Later we had a letter of thanks. It was fortunate that they had turned the radio off at just the right moment.

The closing theme of the Early Birds explained the program. They always signed off with "Keep On Smiling—When you're smiling ...the whole world smiles with you."

"Early Birds". Standing lt. to rt.. Bob Large, Bill Brown. Sitting Lt. to rt. Les Peppin, John Adams and Syd Kennedy.

I remember that at that time, I was in charge of three programs: "Women at Home", "The Sleepy Town Express" for children, and a talent show, and I also remember how my Dad kept constant watch on the station. Wherever he went, he would tune in to see that everything was in order. He would catch us doing all sorts of unauthorized things as most of us were young and irrepressible and sometimes we would utter unwise statements on the air. A gentle word from him was all that was needed. He had a genuine feeling for his staff and I remember one bitterly cold night he tuned in after the station had signed off and hadn't been turned off. He was worried when he couldn't get anyone there on the telephone, and he could still hear the carrier signal. Finally he jumped in his car and drove out of town through drifting snow to the transmitter site. There he found his Chief Engineer, John Q. Adams asleep on the couch. He liked the scrappy little engineer and he covered him gently with a blanket, turned off the transmitter, shut the door and went home to bed.

One very popular person who used to broadcast from our Brace Block studio was an exquisite, dark-haired, young woman who became known as the Veiled Lady of Mystery. Listeners were invited to send in a question about something they had lost—keys, a pet, or perhaps even a sweetheart. As long as their letter was accompanied by a Gastronox boxtop—Gastronox was a patent medicine designed to aid indigestion, flatulence, and constipation—she would use her psychic powers to tell them were to find it. Les Peppin worked with her. He would open the letters, rattling the paper in front of the mike to reassure listeners that no hockus-pockus was going on. She was so beautiful and dressed so smartly that she gave the young men palpitations. Keith Morrow recalls how one steamy, summer's night he was varnishing the studio floor. Believing himself to be the only person in the building, he stripped down to his shorts. A knock came at the door, and thinking it was one of the guys, he flung it open only to confront the lovely Veiled Lady of Mystery. His embarrassment was so acute he slammed the door shut in her face. A short time later, a letter came from the national network advising caution in the use of clairvoyants and psychics, and the Veiled Lady eventually vanished from the airwaves.

Local interest and public service programs were considered to be of the utmost importance at CFCY. It was a firm belief of Dad's that if a community broadcasting station was truly servicing its people, it was bound to have the character of the people it served. He had very strong convictions about how radio should **not** be used, and these could be summed up in the fact that radio **should** be used in the interests of democracy and for the cultural reinforcement and development of its community. This is why he always encouraged suggestions and new ideas.

In the Fall of 1939 the Nazis occupied Holland. It was decided that Princess Juliana of the Netherlands for her safety, would reside in Canada for the duration of the war. One day in the summer of 1941, a top secret communique came into the station from Ottawa. The Princess, who was staying at Pictou Lodge, in Pictou, Nova Scotia wished to record a message of hope and encouragement to the Dutch people to coincide with birthday greetings to her mother, Queen Wilhelmina who was still in Holland. The message was to be broadcast later over short wave. CFCY was selected to make the recording.

Mother and Dad at that time were in New York on holiday. Bob Large and I had been married that spring and were living in Sackville, New Brunswick after Bob began working at the Canadian Broadcasting Corporation's station CBA. My sister Marianne had taken over my job at the station and was broadcasting as Molly Parker on the "Women at Home" program, and doing the "Sleepy Town Express" program for children. Art McDonald was in charge.

Marianne Rogers, later Mrs. A. Keith Morrow.

When the communique came through, it was impressed upon Art that there was to be absolutely no publicity about this visit, the reason for the secrecy being that if the Princess could quietly slip into the Island and out again, she would avoid making her visit official which would require her calling on the Lt. Governor and partaking in functions demanded by protocol. A closed circuit line was set up with Ottawa.

On the day she was to arrive, my sister Marianne and Art McDonald drove out the then gravel road to the Wood Islands Ferry to meet her. The Princess came over in a very ordinary car accompanied by the Lady-in-Waiting, her rather pompus Private Secretary, and a driver who doubled up as a discreet bodyguard. She was pregnant with the daughter who was born later in Ottawa.

As you can imagine there was great excitement around the studio, an excitement heightened by the clandestine nature of the whole affair. There was much discussion over the correct protocol. No one was sure, even, how she should be addressed. Marianne visited Mrs. DeBlois, the wife of a former Lieutenant-Governor, for advice, who said, "Oh, I don't know dear…just act yourself that's what I always did." Eventually, after doing his research, Art issued instructions to the women to give a slight curtsy. The men were to bow. Juliana herself, however put everyone at ease by saying, "While I am in your country, to you, I am 'Yust Yulianna.'" With charm and ease she shook hands and chatted briefly to everyone. The Secretary, though, put them all on edge with his stuffy manner. While Juliana was in the studio making the recording, the bodyguard, who was obviously well armed, cut a very intimidating figure as he paced up and down in the hall outside the receptionist's desk.

Lunch had been arranged at the Charlottetown Hotel. The Secretary, who had talked on the telephone with Art, gave him strict instructions that the lunch had to be in a private dining room. Mr. Arthur Mould, the hotel manager had arranged for everything to be served in the "Royal Suite" on the top floor. When the Princess, the Lady-in-Waiting, the stuffy male secretary, and the bodyguard/chauffeur who loomed ominously in the background, and Marianne and Art were going up in the elevator, a heated discussion took place between the secretary and Juliana.

It was in Dutch, of course, but Marianne imagined it went something like this:

"Where are we going?" asked the Princess.
"To lunch, Highness" responded the Secretary.
"But I saw the diningroom on the way in." "We are going to
dine privately, Highness."
"I wish to dine publicly."
"But your Higness, your identity must be protected—and
perhaps it is more fitting—"

At this point the Princess uttered what was obviously some expletive and stamped her royal foot. The matter ended there. The secretary bowed his head, signalled "down" to the operator, and down went the elevator. Art rushed ahead and informed the manager and they were ushered into the dining room. No doubt the waitresses quietly passed the word to people they knew that there was royalty in the room. This, plus the ostentatious behaviour of the secretary who beckoned and called staff and flashed his gold cigarette case and lighter, soon made them the centre of attraction.

On the way back to the ferry, Art and Marianne led the way in their car while the Princess's car followed behind. They had left it a bit late because before they left Charlottetown, Juliana had insisted they take a turn around the city to see the sights. Rushing for the ferry is a way of life for Islanders, so Art stepped on the accelerator expecting Juliana's car to do the same. But when the dust of the gravel had settled, he soon realized the road behind him was empty. The royal car never went beyond a certain speed—slow. Eventually Art saw them poking along, and he hailed down the dour driver. Art explained that perhaps it would be better if he rushed ahead with someone from the party and arranged to have the boat delayed until they got there. Juliana ordered the secretary to go with Art and Marianne rode in the royal car to make sure the driver didn't take a wrong turn.

The Captain agreed to hold the boat and issued instructions that the Princess's car was to drive straight on. All the other passengers were forced to remain in the line-up until the Princess arrived. When people were given the reason for the delay there were no complaints except from a large vocal gentleman who bitterly commented that if this was his country it wouldn't be tolerated.

After Juliana's visit the office routine slowly returned to normal. Dad offered his service to the War Office in 1940 and was assigned reserve duty as Commanding Officer of the No. 6 Signals. They were an active enthusiastic company which included most of the male members of the CFCY staff. Before the war had ended about ninety men had gone through its ranks into the regular service. As young announcers and operators left the station to go to war, new staff had to be quickly trained. Throughout the war we got the news first hand, of course, and its impact was both terrifying and joyous, as we learned of the reversals and triumphs.

In the spring of 1941, Charlottetown and Summerside became the sites of two of the Commonwealth Air Training bases. Because their own air fields were overcrowded and in constant danger of attack, the British Air Force sent thousands of men to train in Canada. RAF No. 31, General Reconnaissance School was established four miles from Charlottetown on the Brackley Point Road. Summerside trained pilots; Charlottetown trained navigators, observers and gunners.

The men were from all parts of the Commonwealth, most of them, so far from home, were very young—even as young as seventeen. The Islanders, with many of their own young men off in the forces, did their best to make the airmen welcome by taking them to their homes. Dad would pick up young airmen and bring them home to dinner, or take them fishing. My husband Bob and I, after three years at CBA, were by then back at CFCY. We had just had a baby daughter, Brenda, and

Vivian
MacPhail

During war years, girls took on duties as studio operators. The old control rooms were complicated affairs compared to the new, all-computer controlled studios. Wanda MacMillan could "make things fly" in the control room. Later, she was joined by Ethel Kelly and Vivian MacPhail. Doris Hillion was in charge of radio continuity.

I remember one young man, lonely for his wife and newborn son whom he had never seen, wanted nothing more than to hold the baby and walk back and forth, back and forth across the floor with her.

At that time we had a request program during which people would ask for favourite records to be played for loved ones. It was especially popular with the servicemen because requests came for them from overseas and from newly made sweethearts on the island. Word came from Ottawa to "cease and desist broadcasting CFCY request program immediately." Apparently spies had been sending hidden messages through requests for such songs as "Red Sails in the Sunset" and "Three O'clock in The Morning" to the ever-present U-Boat packs lurking in the Gulf of St. Lawrence ready to torpedo the vital North Atlantic Patrol convoying between Halifax and Britain with troops and supplies. The request program was a great morale booster, and it was sadly missed.

Later, CFCY had a part to play in getting the new navigators back to base when they were in trouble. Often they would be far out over the Gulf of St. Lawrence on late night operations as they carried out reconnaissance flights against U-Boats. Foul weather, snowstorms or fog would blanket the Island. Both CFCY and CBA, Sackville, operating at a higher power than the Air Force, would stay on the air sometimes sixteen or seventeen hours so that the navigators could take bearings. Quite frequently our transmitter was on until early morning as our signal "homed" the lost men and planes back to their hangars.

Evelyn Cudmore was host of "Live Longer" water safety program. She was the only person who ever taught Swimming by Air.

Mrs. Fred Osborne talked to lone Guides from Labrador and Newfoundland to Northern Maine.

Chapter Fourteen

Gathering
All
the News

The news on both radio and television comes to us now from centralized points, at lightening-like speed through the use of satellites. Fifty years ago the gathering of news and its dissemination to different radio stations was in its infancy.

CFCY collected the news in a multitude of inventive ways. There was no news-gathering organization whose service we could obtain. On the "Outports Program" Dad, and later Art McDonald would ask listeners to alert the station about news-worthy events. "Flo" Fitzgerald who ran the "Home Forum" program would gather news as she went her rounds selling commercial announcements, and Bill Brown, our first reporter, would cover news on the Island and in Nova Scotia. Many items would be clipped from the newspapers and re-written and world news would be prepared from short wave broadcasts. Almost everyone who worked at the station can recall being involved in gathering news. Wild-eyed staff members or friends would rush in to tell of a fire or an accident happening not far away and ordinary citizens would drop in with a tale of local intrigue and ask to see the Colonel. It might or might not make the news.

I remember once the telephone rang while we were having lunch at home. A caller from the eastern part of the province reported that the famous dirigible R-100 would be passing north of Charlottetown shortly. The ship was on its maiden trip to North America. The lunch was left sitting on the table as we all piled into the car and followed this majestic airship as it glittered in the sun and finally passed out of sight. Another day, just at dawn, we were on hand to wave and shout as two trans-Atlantic flyers, Errol Boyd and Harry Connors took off in their small plane to fly the Atlantic. Several days before, they had made an emergency landing at the foot of Tea Hill halfway up the slope. They thought this would make a good take-off place when the weather cleared and they could resume their flight. They did get across the Atlantic, the eighth recorded crossing, but they just made it, out of gas, landing on a tiny Island off the British Isles.

This was the type of news my father would write up and there were plenty of items too about lost children, dogs and other pets. The time of arrival of the Borden Train, our main transportation link to the rest of Canada, was always a highlight of the news as it would quite often be hours late due to winter storms. The funeral announcements at the end of the news would call for absolute silence in most homes.

The people of Prince Edward Island get really involved in elections. The election of 1935 was no exception. My father usually tried to give non-partisan and fair coverage of both parties, but this time an old friend, Liberal Walter Lea, was in the running to become Premier again. Lea was ill at his home just outside the village of Victoria. He asked my father if he would attempt to broadcast a speech from his home.

Now, a broadcast from a rural district as far away from Charlottetown as Victoria had not been attempted before. It would require the taking over of the one telephone line from Crapaud to Victoria and beyond, a line that served twenty or thirty families. They would all have to agree to stay off the telephone while Walter Lea was speaking. It was a tricky situation, as there were both Conservatives and Liberals on that rural line. I remember driving out there with my father while he personally called on every one of the telephone subscribers to ask for their cooperation.

Normally, it would have been likely for the anti-Lea forces to break in on the line and ruin the broadcast. But Walter Lea was an exceptionally popular man, the first farmer to have been elected Premier of the province. Everyone gave their promise to keep the line open. Lea won the election with a clean sweep of all 30 seats—an unprecedented victory to that time 1935—and the victory speech from Lea's bedside was a success, the first remote broadcast of this type attempted by CFCY.

Dad realized that we needed a special place for the news department when we moved to the Brace Block. He and Art talked it over. Art

McDonald was one of those individuals who saw the ideal finished product and then drove himself and everyone around him towards its completion. Like most who work this way, his life was full of frustration because the ideal is never achieved. This frustration made him prone to outbursts of bad temper and impatience. He was as neat as a pin, and if things around him were disorderly it enraged him. Art's hobby was finished carpentry, and apparently he turned out some very fine work, so he felt confident he could direct someone to get the news department underway.

True to the tradition of all announcers working their way up from the bottom, meaning they had to sweep floors as well as announce and operate, Art put two of the newest novices, Syd Kennedy and Keith Morrow, to work building partitions to enclose the newsroom.

"Okay, now boys there's the tools and the two by fours and the layout for the partitions. Now these will be seen by the public so make sure they're square and plumb." Art warned.

The boys got to work. Later Art came in to inspect.

"What's the matter with you guys? Don't you know what straight means? Look at that, its listing at about thirty degrees, and the whole damn thing is about as straight as a dog's hind leg. Tear it all down and do it again—*right* this time!" Art spat at the announcers and glared at them with contempt.

Syd Kennedy's hot young blood boiled, and he flung his hammer in protest with great force at the offending partition.

"You're fired", roared Art.

"Does that mean both of us?" asked Keith Morrow, not being very experienced in the ways of the world. Art's eyes shot sparks at them. "Yes! Yes! YES!. Get out of here—both of you!"

The boys took off in high dudgeon down to White's restaurant just below the station. Tom White, known by everybody as the "Deacon", a fight promoter among other things, always listened to their tale of woe.

"You guys'd better watch out for the Colonel," the Deacon advised, "He comes in here about this time for his smokes."

And sure enough, just as he was finishing saying it, in walked the Colonel.

"What are you boys doing down here at this time?"

"We're fired, sir."

"What for?"

117

"The carpentry didn't please him."

"Humph" Dad grunted and left. In a few minutes, Adele Coyle, his secretary, put her head in the door. "You boys better get back to work. It's time to go on the air."

That was the last they heard of it. I guess they made better announcers than carpenters. Both went on to have very successful careers in broadcasting; Syd Kennedy becoming the CBC's Maritime Regional Director and Keith Morrow director of several CBC regions from the Prairies (Winnipeg) to Newfoundland and the Maritimes. At one time in the late 1950's he was Director of the English networks and the Toronto area.

The next day the partitions were half up, the hammer still lying on the floor where Syd had flung it, so my father called in George Morrison to do the job. His son came with him. George Sr., was George Lloyd Morrison, and his son was christened Lloyd George Morrison. To save confusion, we called them "old George" and "young George". They became important cogs in the organization, building everything needed from cupboards, partitions and studios to two entire transmitter buildings. George Morrison Sr. had been "Boss carpenter" in the building of St. Dunstan's Basilica in Charlottetown, the largest church on the Island and on many large construction jobs in the New England States.

The first day "young George" came to work, Dad remarked, "You've got a smart boy there." The answer shot back, "He should be. He taught me everything I know and then I learnt a little bit myself". He talked that way. He was crusty and cantankerous with those he didn't approve of and open-hearted with those he liked. Some said he acted as if he was the real boss of the place. I remember when he was in his middle seventies he had an apartment on the third floor of our studio building. We always felt that if we were invited up to visit George and his wife, it was the supreme test of acceptance. I can still see old George yet with his glasses perched on the end of his nose, head forward, inspecting some detail of his work. If the detail happened to be too small, he reached into his pocket without averting his gaze, took out a second pair of glasses and put them on **over** the first. My father read the news himself in the early days of CFCY, but as newscasts became more frequent, regular announcers would be scheduled. Moore & McLeod Ltd. sponsored the noon news for many decades. The evening news was sponsored by Enterprise Foundry Ltd. of Sackville, N.B. for almost as long a period.

When Art McDonald arrived at the station, he sold the Sunday evening news to Blue Ribbon Tea, and he took a personal interest in doing this broadcast himself. To this day, older listeners remember these Sunday night newscasts.

But the person I recall most vividly on newscasts was Stuart Dickson. His was the voice we heard during the war years. Because of his English-accent and his voice of authority, many listeners would not believe the news unless they heard Stuart Dickson read it. He had attended the famous Westminster school in London. In the first World War he served with the East Surrey Regiment and came under gas attack in the trenches in France. Taken prisoner in 1918 he was repatriated after the Armistice. Just before the Second World War he came to work at CFCY and especially when he was relating news about Allied advances or defeat, his former experiences were reflected in his voice. It was compassionate and compelling. He would deliver about six newscasts a day during wartime and when there were special bulletins, he would be heard more often. It was Stuart Dickson who announced the

Courtesy of Wanda Bourgeau

A. Stuart Dickson brought news of victory and defeat. World war II.

allied victory at the end of the war. I remember this tall, transplanted Englishman during the thirty years that he was the senior newscaster at CFCY. He had come to Canada for his health. He was kindly and courteous and he walked with the grace of the expert tennis player, for he soon became the Island Tennis Champion. When Stuart married Agnes Sherrin of Crapaud and settled down here, he produced and directed operettas and plays.

He was a professional through and through and spent much time preparing and rehearsing the news prior to going on the air.

Earlier, we had received a very limited service of bulletins from The Canadian Press, but this was not extensive enough. We needed more news so my father purchased Transradio Press service. This was sent out from New York by wireless in Morse Code and had to be transcribed. It was the first service available to us, and it was awkward and unreliable as the transmissions would be interrupted by weather conditions and static. The Chief Engineer Merrill Young and his assistants Mac Balcolm and Max Corkum all were proficient Morse Code operators but they were beginning to rebuild the transmitter and Transradio Press was moved into the city studio in order to give the transmitter staff more time. Eddie MacLennan was hired as operator. When Eddie left to join the Ferry Command, Les Peppin transcribed the news for a time, but he too left for wartime service with the Department of Transport and once again my father was looking for an operator. The problem was solved when a young girl, Nora Downe, heard about the job. She had learned the Morse Code as a Girl Guide and had no idea that this was a position that women didn't normally fill. It was at the beginning of the war. She was put to work immediately.

The apparatus she used was called a Vis-a-Sig. It was a visual indication of a signal and it responded to the sound of the Morse Code characters and printed them. A pen would write on a ticker tape that crossed over the top of the typewriter and would mark down little pointed high places for dots and long bars for dashes. In the early war years, Nora would transcribe important news from this machine. At times the static would wipe out the transmission and then she would either leave a large space for Stuart Dickson to figure out, or "just fill in the gaps herself!" I remember hearing Nora say recently,

"Everyone was underpaid. I made $7.50 a week, and finally got up to $16.50 a week. Now girls have apartments, run cars, have clothes and serve wine. We all worked for the love of it. I would have done anything to have worked in radio".

Nora had times when there was nothing to do. She sang in the choir and played the piano, so she was able to help Charlie Chamberlain with his songs. He was unable to read music and learning a new song took time and patience. We'd watch Nora and Charlie on the piano bench. She was pretty and Charlie used to tease her. He'd keep getting closer and closer, finally almost crowding her off the end of the bench.

When British United Press became our news source around 1942, it came in on teletype ready for broadcasting, and Nora then became my father's secretary. When we started to use BUP we would see one now well-known person occasionally. Knowlton Nash, a veteran of CBC TV news, was BUP representative in the Maritimes in those years.

Courtesy of Wanda Bourgeau

In the newsroom. Lt. to rt. Stuart Dickson,
Charles MacArthur, J.T. "Mickey" Place.
Back row Jack Morris.

Listening casually, you might get the idea that announcing is easy. Usually the ones who sound effortless are the announcers who really work at it. Charles MacArthur was one of the most thoroughly rehearsed newscasters I can remember. He got his first job at CFCY doing station calls, "This is CFCY, Charlottetown", in a deep, melodious voice.

The Second World War interrupted his career. As a navigator in the Air Force, he dreamed of becoming a radio announcer. He was back after the war, becoming a newscaster and later Sales Manager. His sales ability was demonstrated in England when he persuaded Eve, his wife, to live on Prince Edward Island, a place she had never heard about, after knowing her for only ten days.

At least one person was influenced to become an announcer after hearing Charlie:

Manager, Radio Station CFCY   *Memphis, Tenn.*
Charlottetown, P.E.I.   *U.S.A.*

Dear Sir:

In Memphis yesterday, I saw a bumper sticker that brought back memories of thirty years ago. It said CFCY 630 on the dial.

I was in the U.S. Air Force stationed in Newfoundland. My buddies and I used to listen to CFCY. The best announcer I ever heard was a gentleman by the name of Charles MacArthur. After hearing him I decided I would go into radio after the war. I hope to be able to tune you in again some day.

                                   Sincerely,

                          John M. Crowe

Many other young people who listened to CFCY were motivated to try out for an announcing job. There were summer replacement jobs for University students and many realized that the experience gained could lead them into other occupations or simply help pay for their education. George Hart, well before the fifties, was one I remember who worked in radio and later became a teacher at University in Montreal writing books on his specialty, history. Murray Fraser of Halifax and David MacDonald of Charlottetown started their careers at CFCY while going to college. Murray Fraser going into law and later becoming Dean of the Law School at Simon Fraser University in British Columbia. David MacDonald into the Ministry into politics becoming a cabinet minister and later Canadian Ambassador to Ethopia.

David started in a small way. "I was always interested in broadcasting", he told me. "I decided when I was seventeen that whatever I was going to do, working at a radio station would be a very interesting job, and I began during summer vacations. It was a very informal arrangement but I do remember how much I was paid. It was twenty-five dollars a week and that was big money in the spring of 1954. It was a King's ransom. My eyes were as big as saucers! After learning the basics of the control room, I was allowed to say, 'CFCY in Charlottetown, 630 on your radio dial' or 'This is the friendly voice of the Maritimes, CFCY.' This was very, very exciting to me to think that I would be

When CFCY TV opened, Eric Jessome produced his already popular talent show, "Amateur Cavalcade".

allowed to say something on the air. I remember Lorne Finley trained me and I remember my first radio program was "Saturday Record Time" and I even remember the theme...Larry Clinton's version of "The Dippsy Doodle", an old recording from the 1930's.

Right after it there was the Shur Gain Amateur Cavalcade with Eric Jessome, a most popular program. Ches Cooper would come in and act as MC for it.

I think it was the second summer that I did my version of Rawhide. He was called 'Yukon Ike'. There were stacks of really old records stored in the newsroom. They were heavy and some were only one-sided and we had only one turntable that would play them. I remember they had the grooves going up and down instead of side to side. They were left over from the 1920's. Well, I had a program on Saturday morning and called it, "The Good Old Days" with this crazy impersonation.

I got lots of letters, some for and some against, but one day Bob Large, who was the Manager, decided to have a little fun with me. Gordon Tait was my operator and he gave Gordon a sound effects record with machine gun fire on it. When the noise came on my earphones, I knew I was being attacked so I immediately made up a skit how the radio station was under attack and I was being shot at, and we carried this on for a few minutes. Right after that I went on vacation for a couple of weeks and the program went off the air. I don't know if the people rejoiced because they thought I had been put out of my misery or not, but that was the end of my Saturday morning broadcasting. I did enjoy recording and once I had the opportunity of recording The Leslie Bell Singers, the whole of their concert, and Leslie Bell gave us permission to make it into a presentation for broadcast. That to me was very rewarding. To be able to be creative with broadcasting like that was very exciting. To start at a small station where people know you a bit and trust you and will let you be creative and do different things, that is an advantage."

There were many advantages for those who wanted to learn about radio and one of these was learning to do newscasts. It was the importance given to our newscasts that got us into trouble with the newspapers.

Generally there was little love lost between the newspaper industry and radio. True there were a few farsighted publishers who saw the potential of radio and wasted no time getting into the business. But mainly, due to the threat to their advertising revenue, the newspaper industry which had larger reporting staffs to maintain, feared the new medium.

In the early 1920's the Government of Canada paid little attention to radio, with the exception of the granting of licences and the supervision of the technical aspects of broadcasting by the Department of Marine and Fisheries. At this time, however, religious sects began to seek out broadcasting licences and to use the stations for religious propaganda. Letters of protest bombarded the Members of Parliament in Ottawa and appeared in newspapers throughout the country. The Government became alarmed, and the issue was aired in the House. Coincidental to the religious programs there were also letters protesting the amount of American programs being listened to in Canada. In December of 1928, the Liberal Government of MacKenzie King commissioned Sir John Aird, Mr. Augustin Frigon, and Mr. C.A. Bowman to study and make recommendations on the future of broadcasting in Canada. The Aird Commission, as it was called, conducted hearings throughout the country.

To understand the Commission you would have to look at the backgrounds of its three members. Its Chairman, Sir John Aird, was President of the Canadian Bank of Commerce. Quite early in the proceedings he made the gauche statement that he'd "...once owned a radio but later threw the damn thing out." Mr. Bowman, Editor of the Ottawa Citizen, was well known for his anti-broadcasting stand and made no bones of the fact that he believed broadcasting stations should be owned by a consortium of daily newspapers. Augustin Frigon, Director of Montreal's L'École Polytechnique, was destined to become the General Manager of the Canadian Broadcasting Corporation, years later. The Aird Commission finally recommended a totally nationalized broadcasting system similar to that set up in Germany and Britain. The newspapers threw their support behind it while the private broadcasting station owners including my father, opposed it vigourously. In the next federal election, the Liberals were overwhelmingly defeated by R.B. Bennett's Conservatives. The Aird Report, ominous for those in private broadcasting, was still awaiting adoption by the House.

Dad wrote a long letter to R.B. Bennett giving his views on the report and, generally, "putting him into the picture" as far as Canadian broadcasters were concerned. No doubt the Prime Minister received similar letters from other broadcasters. "RB" wrote Dad personally saying how astounded he was at the revelations he had received and stated that it was his intention to have the report re-studied. Later, he reassured Dad that as long as he was in power, there was "...no chance the Aird Report would be dug out, let alone implemented."

If the Prime Minister thought it was going to be an easy job to bury the file containing the Aird Report, he was mistaken. There were two powerful factors he yet had to contend with: Graham Spry, the founder and head of the Canadian Radio League, and the Canadian newspaper industry. During this time, Graham Spry became synonymous with Canadian nationalism. He and other members of the Canadian Radio League were strongly opposed to American domination of Canadian radio and were convinced that the only way to keep radio Canadian was to nationalize it; so, therefore, they wanted the Aird Report implemented. The daily newspapers, of course, agreed with the Aird Report's "no advertising" recommendations and together with the Canadian Radio League they formed a strong and influential lobby. The private broadcasters soon realized that if this powerful lobby was successful it would spell their doom. They drew together and presented their own lobby. Finally, the result was neither complete nationalization nor complete private ownership. In 1932, a bill was passed in Parliament creating a three-member Commission to "...carry on the business of broadcasting in Canada" during which they were to regulate and control privately-owned stations "...so long as these continued to exist."

The Commission, called the Canadian Radio Broadcasting Commission was headed by journalist Hector Charlesworth, who was at that time Editor of Saturday Night, the prestigious Toronto magazine; the Vice-Chairman was Thomas Maher, a forestry engineer who at one time had been a director of CHRC, a private Quebec radio station; the third member was Lt. Colonel W. Arthur Steel who had a vast technical knowledge, and had served as one of Canada's advisors at the Madrid Conference which had set international frequency allocations. The Canadian Radio Broadcasting Commission was the forerunner of the Canadian Broadcasting Corporation which was created about six months after the Moose River Broadcasts in 1936.

For a while the powerful newspaper industry licked its wounds and settled down to coexist with the new medium until the sudden attention given to radio during the Moose River broadcasts caused the old animosity to surface again. The immediacy of the information and the powerful effect of the spoken voice on the imagination eclipsed the print of the newspapers. Also, because of the direct and instant reporting from the site by the eye-witness, the information tended to be more accurate. For example, the day before the actual rescue, a Charlottetown newspaper put out a special edition claiming that the men had been released from the mine, resulting in the bells from Charlottetown's City hall and churches being rung prematurely. Art McDonald rushed to the microphone with the following announcement:

We wish to warn our listeners against misleading news reports being circulated in a special edition of a Charlottetown newspaper now on the streets. This edition claims that the Moose River men have been rescued and states that direct physical contact has been made with their rescuers. This report, printed and circulated several hours ago is by no means confirmed and may be unconfirmed for several hours.

Keep your radio tuned to CFCY for authentic half hour bulletins direct from the mine.

The newspaper men were furious. Their special edition had been rendered null and void, and they were not going to put up with that. In retaliation, scorching editorials were printed condemning the irresponsibility of radio reporting. Dad and Art McDonald hastened to a lawyer and had provisions made to have all rescue announcements made on the air authenticated by declaration and witnessed by a Notary Public.

The owner of one Charlottetown newspaper, the Charlottetown Guardian, Mr. J.R. Burnett, a rather rotund, dour Scot whose word was law, had decided that "radio is bad business for the newspaper business." He called together his editorial staff and issued the following edict, "the word, *radio* must never appear in the columns of this newspaper." And to my knowledge, it seldom did for almost twenty years.

Dad was a man who believed there was not much point in squabbling. He liked Mr. Burnett, and Mr. Burnett liked him. They attended the same church, the Kirk of St. James Presbyterian, they attended Rotary and other social events together, but there was a tacit understanding on Mr. Burnett's part and Dad respected it, that radio did not exist. Dad, to appease the bruised egos of the newspapermen, wrote a conciliatory editorial in which he pointedly used this phrasing, "Radio,

127

as befitting a younger and more humble servant of the public than the newspaper business..." He also instructed his staff that news items announced over the station were to be concluded with, "For further particulars, see your Daily Newspaper". The mind of the old Scot was made up, however, and no amount of appeasement could budge it.

Many, myself included, tried to talk J.R. Burnett out of his adamantine position towards radio but to no avail. Twenty years later, however, CFCY's accountant Mickey Place was successful in making a breakthrough. Mickey thought it would be a good idea if the Guardian published an election score-sheet which could be filled in by the listeners as the results came over the radio.

"What do you think?" Mickey asked Dad.

"Terrific idea, Mickey, but you'll never get The Guardian to go along with it." Dad answered.

"Well, I'll try anyway...do no harm in trying."

"Good luck" from Dad.

Perhaps in addition to Mr. Burnett's determination to have nothing to do with radio, Dad was thinking of the time when Mickey Place was shoved during the fever of election night when he dared to try to use one of The Guardian's adding machines on which results were being tallied for Canadian Press. An apology was exchanged and bygones were bygones; so Mickey, undaunted, called on The Guardian. By this time the Burnett boys, Ian, Bill and Chick (George) were all actively involved in the day to day running of the paper. Chick and Bill liked Mickey's idea, so they went to Ian who was more senior.

"It's a good idea," Ian said, "but I doubt if the Boss will go for it."

As they went into JR's office, the Burnett boys dropped back a little as Mickey put forward his proposal.

"The answer is **no**," Mr. Burnett stated firmly, "and there's no point in continuing this discussion."

On the way out, Mickey received a sympathetic pat on the back from the boys. "Too bad, Mickey. It's a fine idea."

Back at the office Dad was adding his "I told you so" when the phone rang. It was Chick. They had persuaded JR to give his okay. So, the freeze out that had lasted nearly twenty years ended, and seven years of cooperation began — at least at election time. Once and a while, however, between times, radio was acknowledged in the columns of Charlottetown's morning newspaper as it "Covered Prince Edward Island like the Dew."

Chapter Fifteen

The Sleepy Town Express

O ver the past fifty years, we have seen giant steps taken in the technology of industry and business. In the thirties this was just beginning to happen and people like my father realized that in order to take advantage of this burgeoning technology they would have to constantly improve the equipment. In the late thirties, the young engineer who accomplished this for CFCY was Merrill H. F. Young. Born in Lunenburg, Nova Scotia, he eventually joined the technical branch of the Canadian Broadcasting Corporation but for a few years, he was Chief Engineer at CFCY.

When John Quincy Adams waved a jaunty farewell and left for a new career in Montreal, Merrill came from the Northern Electric Company to fill the position. With nervous, compulsive energy and a tremendous technical knowledge, he first re-built the control room and studio equipment. The most modern microphones were purchased and new turn-tables and recording equipment obtained. Art McDonald describing all these changes in the promotion literature, called it "Equipment as modern as tomorrow".

Like a giant heart, the control room regulates the sounds, the pulse of the programs and records the health of the organization. After Merrill was finished rebuilding it, the programs sounded noticeably different. We were now able to record on large sixteen-inch discs, quarter-hour shows or dramatized spot announcements. Back in 1939 we did it "without cost or obligation".

Merrill then turned his attention to the transmitter. By now it was obsolete as we had been using water-cooled tubes and these with their plumbing complications had to be replaced. He designed a transmitter using the new air-cooled tubes. Another native of Lunenburg, Max Corkum, was hired as Assistant-Engineer. It took two years to replace the transmitter, rack by rack, but finally we had a new high efficiency Class B modulation system.

Completely reconstructed inside, the transmitter now needed a classy new front and in the Bruce Stewart Co. they found a local machine shop and foundry well able to do the job. The steel for the front panels was brought in and cut to size. Merrill and Max, having had experience in a well-known foundry in Lunenburg, filed the steel racks and panels to a perfect fit. When it was finished and painted in an autobody shop, it was a professional-looking transmitter with a centre strip running the whole length in deep maroon trimmed with chrome. These old transmitters were not compact like those of today and the overall length was about sixteen feet. Max told me that it was copied from an RCA Victor model, one of the latest designs of that particular time. Merrill and Max were brothers-in-law and a strong family bond existed between them. They relieved the long monotonous hours at the transmitter with some harmless fun.

They persuaded Dad that if they had to be there until one o'clock in the morning to copy news from Transradio Press, they might as well be on the air. Using all the cast-off records from the studio they put on a program of their own for after-midnight listeners. They had gathered up quite an audience when they decided to try something new. Believing that if you played a record, no matter what it was, over and over again, you could create a hit, they decided to demonstrate this. They picked the worst possible song. "I still remember it", Max declared. "It was called, 'When The Soup Begins To Droop Down Father's Vest' and we played it over and over again using ficticious names for people we said had requested this particular selection. Then we began to get real letters from real people who wanted this perfectly dreadful song played on the air. It became popular—so popular that one time when I was vacationing and went over to Pictou, I stopped at a restaurant and there it was printed on the nickelodeon, 'When The Soup Begins To Droop Down Father's Vest'. It was one way to prove a point".

Max enjoyed the country. He was a teenager and Dad used to take him fishing and hunting. He would drop into the transmitter.

"Come along, Max, I'm going fishing."

"But I can't go fishing Colonel. Don't you remember, I work here".

"We'll soon fix that."

Then the Colonel would phone the studio with a request that they send someone out to replace Max for the afternoon.

"Max is going fishing with me". And that was that. On the way home, they would talk about the affairs of the world, Max relates:

"When I went to CFCY I was just a callow young fellow and I came away a grown up."

The quirk of fate or whatever you want to call it that brought Bob Large and myself back to Prince Edward Island was all mixed up with Merrill. Bob, after being on the original staff of CBA, Sackville, (the 50,000 watt station of the CBC) for three years, had been transferred to Ottawa. I had concluded the weekly broadcasts I was doing under the name of "Jane Weldon" over CBA and our possessions were all packed in boxes addressed to Ottawa when word came that the CBC had acquired the services of Merrill Young, CFCY's Chief Engineer. The telephone rang. It was my father. Would Bob return to take over Merrill's job? He said yes of course and we re-addressed the boxes, and soon found ourselves back on the Island.

I was delighted. I could again resume broadcasting the Sleepy Town Express program for children. My sister Marianne had married Keith Morrow and taken up residence in Halifax when he had joined the Navy. The program was there for someone to organize.

Programs for children started very early in CFCY's history. Mine began in 1925, and in the early 1930's Berna Huestis, a kindergarten teacher (now Mrs. Gordon Schwartz, Halifax), wrote and directed "Betty Ann And the Cuckoo" broadcast on Saturdays. Boys and girls aged four to thirteen would sing songs like "The Little Dustman" and "Cradle Song" and would close the program with something like "Another Perfect Day has Passed Away". The children were chosen for their musical ability and many future choir members and musicians got their start on this program.

We also carried the popular Maritime program "Uncle Mel" conducted by Hugh Mills and sent to us on the very large transcriptions from Halifax, and we had our own local programs "Teen Age Book Parade" and "Saturday Merry- go-round", both produced by Nellie Bryanton Brown during the years 1954 to 1960.

Nellie called herself "Bea Brown" and the programs were alive with ideas as this popular school teacher would gently lead her listeners into the subject chosen. The plays were original and Ruth Boswell contributed the music. Claiming to have "always been nervous before a broadcast" Mrs. Brown remembers one program when the men on the other side of the control room window were laughing so hard they couldn't keep their minds on the program and she couldn't understand why. In the play, "The Clown With the Broken Heart" a whistle was required to be blown every time the clown would speak. At the last moment she had rummaged around the house and found a Girl Guide whistle that unfortunately had a very shrill sound. Arriving at the studio she asked the operator to listen over the microphone to see if the whistle would be alright. When she blew it, it nearly blew him out of his chair.

"Don't ever do that again...you'll blow the whole system to pieces!" he said.

"Then what can I do?"

"Well, you should be back as far as that window at the back of the studio."

By this time she had taken off her shoes, the better to run in stocking feet. There she was, running to the back of the studio, blowing her whistle and running back to the mike all the time desperately trying to find her place in the play. The control operators laughed all the time she was on the air that day.

These programs were a way of educating children about well-loved books and were enjoyed by grown-ups as well as the children. I remember that every city school was involved and hundreds of young people took part.

The children's program I knew most about was The Sleepy Town Express. In fact my alter-ego is the Story Teller. I find it difficult to write about this imaginary character who used to talk to a four-inch elf called "Little Nose" and to a duck called "Jennifer". The Story Teller has travelled on excursions through time and space by way of a Magic Machine and at Christmas she talked to Santa Claus. She has been with me since I was twelve and we were on the air together for over forty-five years.

It started out quite naturally back in 1925 when broadcasts were simple affairs without music or sound effects. The fact that the voice could be broadcast and picked up on a receiving set fifty or sixty miles away was a phenomenal event.

My first broadcast, a radio telephone program as they were called then, was on a carbon microphone developed from an early telephone. I was only twelve and in Miss Mary Irving's Grade Seven class in Prince

Street School. My father was experimenting with his wireless transmitter and he had to have someone to read while he adjusted the equipment. Most evenings I read stories to my young brother Bill before he was put to bed, and Dad got the idea that here was readily accessible talent right under his nose. He ran a long cable down the hall to my bedroom from his own wireless room at the back of the house and placed the microphone in front of us. During those early broadcasts there were very few receiving sets on the Island and people would travel many miles just to hear a broadcast. We had no idea how many people were listening. After school I would climb over the railing of the second-floor balcony, loosen some slats and squeeze into a space about six feet square on the slanted roof of the downstairs porch and there I would practice out loud. Mary Irving and Jessie Fullerton, teachers at the school, found material for me. Later when CFCY had a studio downtown, we added music. There was the sound of a train puffing into the station and the words:

"We're going to meet Jack, we're going to meet Jill,
They live in a shack on Pumpkin Pie Hill
.....and the Sandman dear is an engineer
On the Sleepy Town Express."

That train became my theme song and the program was called "The Sleepy Town Express".

It was pure fantasy. A place children could escape to when things bothered them or when they just wanted to sit quietly and listen to a story. It was a world of the imagination where children were asked to "look for your pretenders in the bottom drawer of the old chest" and they would hurry to put them on because "Little Nose" and "Jennifer Duck", the "Snow Fairy" and "the Bubble Fairy" and all the characters who peopled our times on the air would be along to talk to them.

Bill Brown, later to become well-known as a sports announcer, was "Conductor Bill" and Ralph "Kelly" Morton, first resident representative of The Canadian Press in Charlottetown, became "The Old Scribble Man". I remember we called him an ancient scribe whose long white whiskers were always found dipped in an ink well. Today's children would hardly know what ink wells were for, but in the middle

133

twenties they were an important part of every child's school desk.

The first Santa Claus voice belonged to Bill Fitzgerald and was heard on the Home Forum Program run by his mother, "Flo" Fitzgerald during the noon hours. When I started writing in the part of Santa Claus, I asked Jim Crockett, a tall, solidly built man with a very deep voice to do it. He was an executive of Holman's, the department store that was my sponsor. He was a compulsive worker and soon was writing his own material. He became completely wrapped up in the program—so much so that he kept a scratch pad beside his bed to mark down any inspirational material he might think of during the night. I believe there was also one beside his tub. He lost sleep and regretfully he had to give it up. Ruby Houle, an experienced actress with the Charlottetown Little Theatre, played "Mrs. Santa" and she suggested J. Austin Trainor for the role of Santa.

Mr. Trainor was a short, bouncy man, rotund with twinkly blue eyes. He was perfect for the part. He was also an experienced actor and had known many famous people while travelling on the Keith Vaudeville circuit as a member of the Dochsteeder Minstrel Show. After coming back home, he directed plays for the League of the Cross Drama Society and produced the yearly St. Patrick's Day Play as well as the Easter Monday Play and the annual Minstrel Show for the Holy Redeemer Parish. His daughter, Leona Sinclair remembers past St. Patrick's Days:

> *My father would always send my mother, Patricia, a bunch of shamrocks on St. Patrick's Day and we children, two boys and three girls, had to dress in green that morning when we went to school.*
>
> *In the afternoon, we would attend the St. Patrick's Day play produced by my father. It was the biggest day of the year. They practiced at our house and I remember one play where they used a big sheet of tin to make thunder. That was exciting."*

By 1938, Austie Trainor had produced his 547th entertainment, "The Sunshine Girl" in aid of the Charlottetown Hospital. He was one of the first to receive the Canadian Drama Award but he always thought of the children first. He would never tell anyone that he was playing the part of Santa Claus. Even the famous actor's publication "Billboard" referred to a "character part" he played on the radio. I remember each time he made his appearance, whether it was on radio or television, he would wear his bright red suit and would be using newly washed white gloves courtesy of his darling wife Patricia. He would sing songs in his deep bass voice, accompanied for many years by his own arrangements on his accordian. Later Jackie Doyle played the piano for him. He loved to make up a parody to a tune like "Smile Awhile".

"Fare you well, and goodbye everyone
One more night and my work will be done,
Christmas morn will bring you joy
Joy to every girl and boy
Dream of Santa, all the whole night through
Go to sleep and I will come to you
A Merry Christmas to you all
'Till we meet again."

Courtesy of Gilbert Clements

Santa Claus and his accordian entertain
young listeners in Montague, P.E.I.

135

He would end with a jolly "Ho…Ho…Ho…Ho…Ho…Ho…" and as his voice was coming from the North Pole, we faded it out and only the wind kept blowing.

The children loved him and he in turn loved all of his listeners. He became the authentic grand old man of the North Pole and his voice was the finest for that important role that I have ever heard.

I was away at school for a couple of years and my sister Marianne produced the Sleepy Town Express program with the kind of panache only a teenager can manage. She remembers one lovely spring night strolling slowly toward the studio not thinking about time when to her horror she heard the theme of the program drifting out through an open window. Down the street she flew, coat flapping behind her, and just managed to get in a breathless "Hello boys and girls, this is the Story Book Lady" as the theme finished.

Later when Bob Large and I were married in 1939 and we moved to Sackville, New Brunswick, The Story Book Lady went on the air again. This time it was an "all stops out" production with the help of a young announcer Ira Stewart. Marianne brought her ability as a writer to the expanded half-hour and thousands of children listened raptly to the program. Ira, who later became a Variety Producer for the CBC's ninety minute "County Roads" program from Halifax, spent hours researching music for this early childrens' program.

After I came back I remember that I created characters at will. There were many throughout the forty-five years the program was on the air. Mickey the elf was George Scantlebury for five or six years until one day he grew up and had a voice change. George's voice was so distinctive that we had to give the elf a new name. We called him "Little Nose". Lloyd Shaw was then the Superintendent of City Schools and we found out that playing one of the discs he had made at a different speed produced the right tone of voice and string of chatter that suited the little elf. We used this for a time, but it was too risky. We were afraid that someone might put the recording on at the right speed and the disguise would be disclosed. I don't believe Dr. Shaw ever knew he was on the Sleepy Town Express Program.

Many of the sound effects and much of the music chosen were the work of Loman McAulay. It was Loman who finally recorded the voice of Bev Hatton Murphy as belonging to "Little Nose", the four-inch elf who hid in desk drawers, curled up for a nap in ash trays and spoke a very strange language that very few people could understand. Little

Nose was very real to the children and they would send him presents of tiny sweaters, capes and mittens. There would even be special cakes baked for him. Mary Trainor, Betty King Howatt, and Marlene Balderson played the Bubble Fairy and the Snow Fairy at different times and one of the main characters was "Jennifer Duck" who sounded suspiciously like the famous Donald. Gretchen Walters Schyler was the only one who could do this imitation.

When the program went on television we devised all kinds of gimmicks. There was a small train with elves riding around in it. Doug Wood would sometimes take over for Loman but with a program on the air for that length of time, mostly everyone at the station at one time or another took part in The Sleepy Town Express.

There is a joke in my family that Mom should never open her mouth to speak in public because the Story Teller will pop out and I will be recognized.

Courtesy of Gord Johnston

Gretchen (Walters) Schyler played Jennifer Duck.

Doug Wood has been with CFCY for 31 years.

137

I remember once going to the home of the Sisters of the Most Precious Blood to buy a rosary that was to be a Christmas present for a friend. The sisters were cloistered nuns and there was no way you could see behind the lattice-work screen. I explained what I wanted and a voice soft like the sound of little tinkling bells answered me. Then I heard "Ohhhhh…" and I thought for a moment I had offended her. I asked apologetically if I had. A delighted laugh came through the screen.

"Oh of course not. I'm just back to my childhood. You must be the Story Teller I used to listen to as a little girl."

Wherever I go I meet former listeners. In Kingston, Ontario recently I ran across a nurse who to my amazement remembered the program. Jean Aitken Strong said that she had listened while growing up in the Magdalene Islands. I often wonder if today's children would appreciate the stories as much now when violence on earth and programs showing clashes in outer space occupy much of the television screen. I honestly think they would. Stories about giants, goblins, witches and elves never lose their appeal.

The Sleepy Town Express was also on television. Carl Sentner on camera. Betty Large, "Story Teller".

Chapter Sixteen

Comings and Goings
CFCY, First Station in the Maritimes
at 5000 Watts

In the year 1941 CFCY was on the air for seventeen hours a day with a power output of 1000 watts. Our full-time staff by this time was fourteen people. The CHCK 50 watt transmitter that my father had purchased from Jim Gesner and his board of directors was used for public service broadcasting only. We had expanded our operations and the rented quarters in Queen Street's Brace Block were becoming too cramped. The ever present urge to develop and improve, to create a modest Prince Edward Island "Radio City" plunged Dad into planning a building designed to facilitate a modern radio station with an efficient business office and studio. One that he would own.

He found a large old home that had been a boarding house next to the Charlottetown Hotel. After a lifetime of improvising and making over, I think he intended, at first, to do all the renovations himself with the help of George Morrison and his son Lloyd. Given the state of the building and what he wanted to do with it—which was to completely redesign it from the bottom up—it soon became apparent that his old way of doing things would not work. Dad could envision how a complex piece of electronic equipment would work out, but when it came to buildings and interiors he could not picture what they would look like when finished. It was not too long before they found themselves in hot water, so an architect, James Harris, was consulted.

Hours of talk later, with ashtrays piled high with cigarette butts and the air blue with smoke, they agreed upon a plan. To help Dad see what it would look like finished, Mr. Harris made a scale model. A year later the old house was completely gutted and rebuilt, its exterior sporting the newest type of glass brick, and CFCY in large letters hanging proudly over the front door—the new station had finally emerged.

On January 24, 1943, there was a gala opening, the only formal opening CFCY had had to date. It was broadcast, of course, with short speeches from the Lt. Governor, the Premier, The Mayor and the presidents of all the local service clubs. It symbolized the culmination of years of perseverance and struggle. I think if Dad were to have chosen the most gratifying moment of his life, that would have been it. It was probably the only time he paused long enough to think of the past and look forward to the future.

CFCY Office and studios Kent Street. Lt. Charlottetown Hotel.

Dad's new office gave him a good vantage point for watching the town go by, and I'm sure as he watched the comings and goings he thought about things which affected the city and the province in general. He was active in the Chamber of Commerce and the Board of Trade, and he devoted hours to talking with other members and friends about how things might have been improved. One man he had a great deal of respect for was Mr. H.K.S. Hemming. Mr. Hemming was a businessman who had retired to the Island. He was slight of stature and very dignified in an Edwardian manner. His immaculate old-fashioned clothes—a bowler hat, a black suit with pearl-grey spats, and a rolled black umbrella—gave him a somewhat eccentric appearance.

Mr. Hemming spent a lot of his retirement time researching the Island, and he drew up masses of maps and documents proving that Prince Edward Island could be an important trade centre. He saw the rich potential the tourist industry held for the Island, not to mention the food industry. Mr. Hemming was a man ahead of his time in commerce, just as Dad was a man ahead of his time in radio. They were kindred spirits and they spent hours in the new office pouring over Mr. Hemming's charts, documents and statistics. Beth MacLaine Cole, who was Dad's secretary at the time said, "After hearing Col. Rogers and Mr. Hemming talking, I went home at night with grandiose ideas about our beloved Island. PEI would be the centre of the world! It would happen because Col. Rogers and Mr. Hemming had said so!"

When his business allowed him more time to himself, Dad bought a hunting dog, an Irish setter named "Roddy". Roddy had a pedigree that stretched for a whole page, legal size, but for all of that, he was a dog with very little brain.

He was affectionate and he was beautiful. His hair was silky fine and burnished red, and when it reached the back of his legs, it curled up in feathery spirals. My father, with great difficulty, taught him to "heel" and he could handle that fairly well, but when it came to fetching partridge from the stubble of a field, or ducks from the slimy weeds along the North Shore inlets, Roddy couldn't seem to get the idea at all. He was sensational though, at fetching things from around the neighborhood: a toy duck, a left shoe belonging to a little boy, or the dainty pink blanket from a baby carriage. These treasures were carried tenderly in Roddy's mouth and laid proudly at my father's feet. The Irish setter's tail wagged furiously, thumping the floor, while he sat on his haunches and begged approval. Then man and dog, under cover of darkness, would steal around from house to house, putting back the loot.

Roddy soon settled in as a mascot around the office, stretching out in front of Dad's desk and sometimes jumping up on some unwary caller and licking his face. My father was relaxing, but the peace and quiet was only temporary.

Problems emerged from the 50,000 watt broadcasting station CBA having been placed in Sackville, New Brunswick by the Canadian Broadcasting Corporation. My father always felt that it would jeopardize the operation of CFCY through a loss of audience and a loss of morale. There was also great danger that CFCY would be cut off the network when the large and powerful 50,000 watts came pounding into Prince Edward Island.

Up to this time, CFCY had been a basic station of the CBC and on the trans-Canada network, and the first blow was that we were placed on the Dominion network, the secondary one for the Corporation. Where we had been the most powerful outlet for Canadian network programs heard throughout the central Maritime provinces, with a population of approximately half a million people, now we would no longer receive the important network programs and the province would suffer as a result. Dad began at once writing long letters and telephoning important people. It was a fight for provincial rights and this time he had the backing of the press and much public support. Even those who had ignored radio for so many years were behind him. It was a hard fight, but provincial prerogatives were being threatened and the press quickly realized that the fight was theirs also.

The result was that we remained on the Dominion network as a basic provincial station but were added to the Trans- Canada network for all major event programming. We found ourselves in an enviable position indeed. Later years proved that CBA as a Maritime outlet was not as harmful to us as it had appeared it would be, and the Dominion network was a successful operation with many popular programs.

CFCY had been established in the new building for about a year, hardly long enough to get used to it, when it became known that private broadcasting stations across Canada would be given permission to increase power from 1,000 watts to 5,000 watts. It was wartime and the Department of Transport had issued a regulation stating that after a certain date, all power allocations would be frozen for the duration of the war. My father felt that we would have to retain if possible the number of listeners we already had, and to do this we would need additional power, but could it be done in time?

Max Corkum had left to join the Navy and Lorne Finley was Assistant to Bob Large, Chief Engineer. Bob did a lot of research and they decided that they might be able to beat the deadline if they could buy some units and assemble them together to make a composite transmitter. The race was on and Lorne began changing the power supply so that higher power tubes could be installed. This took months of work and there were special problems in procuring equipment as manufacturers rightly were alloting it all to the services. When they finally got the parts and turned on the power, some of the capacitors severly overheated and the insulating wax started running out of them. It was a great disappointment to have to return to 1,000 watts. They had to scramble to locate new capacitors but they did manage to beat the deadline and CFCY became the first private station in the Maritimes to go to 5,000 watts power daytime, 1,000 watts at night.

During the war years, the dividing line as to who did what was very blurred, indeed for various staff responsibilities the only objective was to get the job done whatever it was. Bob remembers working at the transmitter in the early morning, later filling in as Program Director because Art McDonald was ill at the time, doing programs and newscasts. After midnight some nights there would be maintenance work on the transmitter. All staff members had to fill many different positions. It was a period of constant changes within the staff.

Even though there was an open and generous atmosphere in the station, the standard of performance was extremely high. In those days either the Colonel or Bob Large, who became Manager and Program Director, had a radio on all the time and no one got away with carelessness or sloppiness. As a result "The Friendly Voice of the

A. Lorne Finley.

Robert F. "Bob" Large

Maritimes" was looked upon as a training ground for announcers and some came for a few years until they got experience. There was pressure to "make something of themselves" in larger centres and they felt that to get anywhere in radio, they would have to be on the move. Added to this was the fact that because of the high standards at the station, their services were looked for by the CBC and larger private stations.

Loman McAulay was one of those who stayed. He liked the Island and never regretted living his lifetime in his own home city. He was on the air for forty-five years, probably a Maritime record for continuous years at one radio station and perhaps a Canadian one as well. He held a wide variety of positions at the station; operator, announcer, sportscaster, emcee and television production supervisor, but he really enjoyed being on the air and he became one of the most successful, durable and popular broadcasters in Eastern Canada.

He was young when he started out.

Loman McAulay.

My mother got me the job. I was barely seventeen and playing in the navy band. The war was on and she thought if I got a job in radio, I'd stay home. Art McDonald hired me in 1942 and the first program I ever announced was "The Merry Makers" a home grown version of what Don Messer did later."

When Loman was eighteen, he confounded his Mother by joining the Navy but after his overseas service he came back to broadcasting. Bill Brown, back from the Army, was covering the races from the Charlottetown Driving Park and Paul Williams and Loman would go along as a team. Art McDonald would do vivid descriptions from the track between heats until 1945, when he became so ill he was unable to do the Old Home Week Races. It was a sad time for everyone. Art wanted desperately to do the races but he was just too weak. He wrote in his daily journal, "Last day at work. Summer, 1945".

John MacEwen and Loman McAulay were sent out to the track to do what Art had always done, "color". Paul was the technician. They described the crowd, the weather, the whole [11]scene in general as well as doing interviews with horsemen and visiting celebrities. Art McDonald had been a master at this and a most popular figure on the air and it was a difficult spot to be in. Art at that time was a patient at the Provincial Sanitorium and they knew he was listening along with thousands of fans all over the Maritimes.

L. A "Art" McDonald.

Most sports events were broadcast. As early as 1928 Dad would pick up WGY from New York and re-broadcast the baseball scores in the World Series. In the early thirties when the Maritime Hockey League was being played, direct broadcasting from the rinks was banned. It was a matter of using your wits to get the information about the games out to fans. As a substitute service, a continuous stream of messages written by an alert reporter were telegraphed to a local newspaper and sent out over the air by CFCY. The commentator in 1931 was J. Buller Murley who handled our earliest sports broadcasts and he was assisted ably by Ed Acorn. The fans even contributed small amounts to cover the costs of the telephone lines and the telegrams in the early days. They'd collect a nickle here, a dime there and sometimes twenty-five cents—a handsome donation at that time. Frank Acorn, Ed's son, collected some of this money and was at The Guardian Office to witness the broadcasts that took place beside a telephone in the hall. He said that Buller would try to make them sound real, as if he was actually in the Halifax rink and when he told about the puck missing the net, one of them would hit the wall with their fists to indicate a dull thud.

Bill Brown, Loman McAulay
Ira Stewart, announcers.
Circa, 1940

Later Bill Brown and Loman would broadcast the hockey games from Truro, Moncton and other centres. Loman developed much expertise in play-by-play commentary travelling to Quebec City and to Detroit for special games. Loman's "they bang it in!" was as widely recognized in the Maritimes as Foster Hewitt's "He shoots, he scores!"

It was Bill Brown who was known far and wide in connection with the Race Track. Bill knew the horses and drivers well, having been taken to the track by his father who was clerk of the course for fifty years. On Wednesdays Bill would always be doing a race commentary either from Charlottetown, Truro, Bridgewater or Pictou. He would describe the race and announce the winner while Loman would do the commentary between heats. Bill got the job in a rather strange way. CFCY had just signed a contract with the Halifax Chronicle to do the Old Home Week Races from Charlottetown and everyone thought that the late Senator Harold Connolly, then the sports editor of the paper, would be coming over to do them. He was surprised to find that he was supposed to do the races as he didn't know any of the horses. Everyone ran to the late Col. Dan MacKinnon with the problem. Just then Bill Brown was coming across the centre field from the barns and Col. Dan looked up and said: "There's your man there". So Bill was asked if he'd whisper the names of the horses into Harold Connolly's ear and they did that for the first few races, and then it got too complex and Bill did the rest of the heats and for many, many years after that, twenty-five to be exact. The MacDonald Tobacco Company presented him with a special plaque honoring his twenty-five years of broadcasting the races.

While Bill Brown Jr. was considered an expert on harness racing, many other voices are well remembered over the years. Art McDonald, Frank "Duck" Acorn, Loman McAulay and in later years, Ed Watters were some of these, all adding their own brand of excitement to the Old Home Week Celebrations from Prince Edward Island known as "The Kentucky of Canada". Loman and Bill's close association on the air came to an end when Bill left to go into business for himself.

It was Loman McAulay who made the early recordings of Don Messer and his Orchestra in our studio in Charlottetown. The discs were cut every two weeks and sent to Decca to be pressed. When Lorne Finley was Chief Engineer, he and his assistant Gordon Tait installed new equipment for the studio and the two new control rooms. The console was a commercial one with many modern improvements. One

147

of these was called "fold back". It was an innovation that allowed the operator to play the recording back to the singer and there would be no "feed back" from the speaker. The singer then would harmonize with the first recording and the two renditions would be mixed into one another. The final result would be the singer harmonizing with herself. Loman said he heard the song "Why Do You Care" and persuaded Marg Osbourne to learn it and Don Messer to put in on his program. Loman recorded Marg singing it first and then on the second recording she sang perfect harmony with herself. It was put out under the Apex label and Loman told me it was the first time the record company had used this technique in Canada and the first time Marg had done it. It was a few years before Patti Page made it popular in the States. Charlie Chamberlain, who sang duets with Marg, was adept at singing harmony, as he had a marvellous ear for music.

I can see the studio where Don Messer did his broadcasts clearly in my mind now, although it was torn down some years ago to make room for a new fire station. The orchestra itself almost filled the studio and the viewing gallery outside would be packed with fans every night they were on the air—three or four tiers of them, all wanting to catch a glimpse of their favourite performers. The walls of the studio were finished in half-circles of bent wallboard because this rather odd-looking effect gave the best reverberation of sound. It was a studio design worked out by Bob Large who was bent on developing the best sound possible from that studio.

It was a fact that all of the station facilities were planned so that local broadcasting could be expanded and more and more local talent was encouraged to take part. We arranged lots of talent shows and I remember the performers well because I was part of the search for talent. I will never forget the sixteen-year-old girl who arrived for an audition. She was bubbly and attractive and she could really belt out a song. She had chosen to sing "My Tiny Little Yellow Polka Dot Bikini". It was a great performance. The only trouble was that that was the only song she knew!

Loman and I used to divide audition nights between us and this was one of his experiences:

"One night I auditioned this girl and fellow. The girl was the singer and he was the guitar player and they also had a bass player with them. I remember writing down 'the girl...beautiful build but not such a good

148

singer' and then I wrote ...'man is a good guitar player.' So after we had finished, the guitar player came back and said: 'would it be possible for me to make a record sometime' and he said, 'I write my own songs'. So I said sure, that's all the better and I made a date to record him the next week and you know, it was Gene MacLellan. The girl was Lena Welsh and she turned out later to be Stompin' Tom's wife. So Gene came in and recorded "Snow Bird", "Robin On Your Window Sill" and two other songs. Snow Bird has two verses in English and one in French because Gene MacLellan is bilingual. It was just before he became famous with "Snow Bird".

At that time Bob Large had asked Loman to record the best of these performers for a station talent Library and we used to put these selections in on our program schedules—at least one new performer each hour. We built up a good local library that way and gave the performers some exposure to the public that they normally wouldn't have had. The recordings were well done. Loman would take great pains with them and there'd be a piano and bass and sometimes a drummer. Because it was local talent it was important. Sometimes I think there is more talent on the Island now and fewer ways for it to express itself. One thing about Bob Large was that he felt that the Manager of a broadcasting station should be interested in and have a close hand in the overall direction of the station's programs which are the end product of the whole effort of running a broadcasting station. In his words, a Manager should not be able to pass the final responsibility off to a Program Director.

The Kent Street office buildings and studios proved a success, although at first it took a lot of persuasion to convince the bank to back Dad, but it was typical of him to take the appropriate risks to put a good idea into action. It was also typical of Dad—to put it mildly—to be haphazard in his day to day accounting methods. But by 1946, business was so good it was apparent to him that he badly needed to hire an accountant, a full time office manager. Which he did, in the form of J.T. "Mickey" Place.

Mickey was an Islander by birth, but like many bright young Islanders he was forced to go elsewhere to seek opportunities. Mickey went to New York where he worked as an accountant. When war broke out he came home and enlisted in the Canadian Army. After the war he returned home to PEI with his wife and child. He wanted to settle here but there did not seem to be many opportunities for someone with

149

his skills and experience. So, he bought a train ticket for British Columbia, planning to try his luck there.

In the meantime, the Army hired Mickey to do an inspection of the No. 6 Signallers, Dad's militia unit. His report was very thorough — so thorough and professional, he got a call saying that Dad wished to see him. It was the day before he was to leave for British Columbia. Thinking it had to do with the inspection report, he went down to see the Colonel. "Look here, Mickey, I'm so impressed with your report on the Unit, I think you are the man I'm looking for. I need an office manager and accountant. Are you interested?" Dad asked a surprised Mickey. Of course, he accepted. It was like an answer to a prayer. He cashed in his ticket to BC and went home and unpacked.

Hitherto unheard of things like production graphs and flow charts appeared. Dad was flabbergasted when Mickey worried when he was two cents out after he had balanced the books. The rigid formality and discipline of the Chase National Bank where he had worked in New York City and the army were a far cry from the casual way Dad ran CFCY. There is one lovely story which I think illustrates the difference between the two men. The first fall Mickey was at CFCY, a friend called him at home one evening and invited him to go shooting. The hunting season opened the next day. Mickey phoned around town and finally located Dad at the Officer's Club — probably arranging his own hunting trip over a drink with his cronies. When he was called to the phone and listened to Mickey's request for time off, Dad was incredulous. He replied:

"I don't give a damn what hours you put in or anything else. I'll let you know if you are not doing your job properly. Until then, take time off to go shooting, everyone expects you to do that."

That was the end of it. Mickey must have tuned into Dad's wavelength, and Dad, no doubt, tuned into his; he stayed with CFCY for twenty-seven years, running CFCY's office loyally and meticulously. After his retirement, he accepted a post at the University of Prince Edward Island as Manager of the Student Union, and was so well thought of, the university conferred an honorary doctorate on him during its Convocation.

Talking about those years, the golden years of radio before television came in, Mickey had this to say:

"When I came to CFCY the programs were scheduled to what one would think would be to the advantage of the listener. The Program Manager and the programs were the dominant concern. Of late years, we've tended to make radio everywhere sound the same. At that time CFCY sounded like CFCY; CJFX over in Antigonish sounded like Antigonish, and the Halifax area sounded like the Halifax area. Now it is very difficult to tell if you are listening to a station in Chilliwack, B.C. or San José, California—they all sound the same."

Chapter Seventeen

Looking Ahead
to
Television

Private radio pioneered Canadian broadcasting. Private enterprise sought broadcasting licenses when they were going begging. Without a penny of subsidy from government (and so without any cost to the taxpayer) individuals across Canada, many of them merely enthusiastic amateurs, laid the foundations of broadcasting in this country. They put up the original transmitting stations, they bought the equipment, they put on the air the best programs they could procure and they did this at a time when radio advertising was virtually unknown and when the operation of a station was a most uncertain enterprise. Like all pioneers, their reward was in hope for the future.

It was this hope that my father was working for in 1946, a very busy year for him. He was President of the Maritime Association of Broadcasters and Hon. President and Vice-Chairman of the Canadian Association of Broadcasters. During the next twelve years the private broadcasters in Canada would be making major breakthroughs in the establishment of today's broadcasting structure. That year my father was a member of a committee presenting a two-part brief on broadcasting to the federal government. Most of the men who planned this brief had been in radio since its inception and all of them were imbued with the conviction that there was an important place in Canada for community-based privately-owned broadcasting.

The opening statement of policy was brief and clear-cut. It said: "we emphasize our belief that, regardless of patterns accepted as suitable for other nations, there should be in Canada: (1) a nationally-owned radio system controlling its own radio stations throughout the country and whatever networks it may deem desirable to fulfill its expressed obligations and (2) a system of independently-owned community stations throughout the country."

The early pioneer broadcasters were highly service oriented and examples cited of public service performed by the private stations in Canada occupied 28 closely printed pages. They also recommended a Radio Board of Appeal and that hearings before such a board would be public hearings.

At that time, the Canadian Broadcasting Corporation had regulatory control over private stations in Canada as well as running their own organization and that was deemed to be unfair. "We submit that no government, with any claim to being democratic, combines in one body the legislative, executive, judicial and police powers."

No one knew better than my father of the long years of community involvement, the financial struggle to survive and the dedication, determination and plain hard work of the private broadcaster and the will to put all this before the Canadian government and the people of Canada occupied his mind.

Those presenting the brief included Guy Herbert of Toronto, Tiny Elphicke, Vancouver, Narcisse Thivierge of Quebec City, Jack Beardall of Chatham, G.R.A. Rice, President of the Western Association of Broadcasters, Phil Lalonde, Montreal, A. Gauthier, Sherbrooke, F.C. Colborne and Keith Rogers, President, Maritime Association of Broadcasters. In the ensuing years the Canadian Association of Broadcasters became firmly committed to having a separate regulatory body and this necessitated many hours spent on planning. Appearing before the Massey Commission and parliamentary committees on broadcasting became of paramount importance and Ottawa became the centre of my father's attention.

While heretofore other parliamentary committees had been harsh and inquisitorial to those appearing before them, the members of the Massey Commission were courteous. All who wished to appear were given equal opportunity to express themselves in an open atmosphere. But rather than solving the disputes ingrained in the system, the report of this commission only tended to fuel the fire raging around broadcasting. The government continued to hold committee hearings into broadcasting in 1950, 1951, and 1953 and throughout, the argument for an "impartial regulatory body" was upheld. Some felt that this issue, a major, often bitter political one involving hours of debate in Parliament, was responsible for the formation of both the Massey and the Fowler Commissions. My father did not live to witness the formation of the Board of Broadcast Governors which was succeeded by the present Canadian Radio-Television and Telecommunications Commission. The BBG was put forward in Parliament in 1958 by the Hon. George Nowlan, Minister of National Revenue at a time when private broadcasting was forty years old.

The new Board was given power to make regulations for both the CBC and the privately-owned radio and television stations. It was Lester B. Pearson who voiced in Parliament what I believe these early pioneers would have been immensely proud to hear:

"We have always said, and we still believe, that the private broadcasters up to today have rendered a very useful service to Canada. In certain instances they could no doubt have improved their standards, as pointed out by the Fowler Commission, but we on this side of the House believe that, in evidence of some deficiencies—and the CBC has also shown evidence of some deficiencies—the private broadcasters now constitute an integral and valuable part of our national system."

In the galleries that day were many of the men who fought hard for equal rights for private broadcasters.

In 1947 my father had begun to have problems with his health. Around Christmas he had a heart attack. He was told to stay home and recuperate. His doctor had been very precise, stern in fact. There would be no more dragging heavy duck decoys into the marshes and no more fishing. He would have to give up smoking. You would find him propped up in bed while dictating a few short letters, no more of the long, lucid, enthusiastic kind he gloried in, just a few short notes.

My mother was more fearful than she had even been in her lifetime, and she adopted a fiercely protective attitude. Where the house had been sunny, full of flowers, interesting people and music from early morning until late at night, it now took on a hushed atmosphere. Shades were drawn and only those with good news were allowed in. People whispered in the hall. This of course was before the years of Dr. Dudley White and his enlightened programs of rehabilitation.

My father's answer to the isolation his heart attack had placed him in, was to turn on his amateur radio transmitter and "chew the rag" with his "ham" friends in distant countries. First he had the help of other amateur operators. Some equipment was moved from the basement to his bedroom and wires, like in the old days, were strung everywhere. He was putting out up to five hundred watts. For an antenna several years before, Dad had searched the Island for the highest tree but could not find one that suited him and with the help of the telephone company, he ordered a large pole from British Columbia. It arrived one day at high noon, tying up traffic for blocks around as the men endeavoured to get it around a corner. It was set up in a deep hole in the middle of Mother's garden. Dad had fibbed a little. It wouldn't be much of a pole, he had told her. She would hardly be able to see it among the trees and shrubs. When it arrived the pole was big and round and ugly. It was nearly fifty feet high. The situation was saved because when my Mother saw it, she was so shocked she couldn't utter a word.

I've been told by Walter Hyndman that Dad was the first amateur ham radio operator in Prince Edward Island but I am not sure there is proof of that. Certainly he was one of the first. He referred to himself as 1HI "One Happy Indian". His cheery voice could be heard calling "CQ....CQ, VE1HI calling CQ....come in anyone...calling CQ...."

He would talk to a "Ham" in South Gate, California and in Derby, England, and to one in Chicago. A log of the cards that came that year were from states all over the U.S.A, but he also talked to such diverse places as Resolution Island in the north and to the R.A.F. base in Rangoon, Burma. Marianne hurried over from Halifax to cheer him up. She found him sitting up in bed in the middle of it all and he told her that amateur radio had "saved his life".

When spring finally came and he heard the wild geese honking as they flew over his house and headed up the West River, he was determined that he would get well, and he took a trip out west to attend the Annual Meeting of the Canadian Association of Broadcasters. On the way he wanted to see the place called Sand Point, Idaho just over the border from Canada, where his father "W.K." and his mother had lived in the early days of their marriage. My brother Bill went with them to do some of the driving. Being true Prince Edward Island people they stopped every once in a while to visit a relative here and one there, and

155

Keith Rogers and amateur wireless station VE1HI. Note early television set. Freak reception only in early 1950's.

Amateur wireless card sent to hundreds of "hams" all over the world.

finally reached Sand Point—a still undisturbed place in the wilderness, a railroad station where "W.K." had sent so many messages by Morse Code along the new railway line to the west.

My father presided at the broadcaster's annual meeting at Jasper Park Lodge, the keynote speaker giving a rousing address to private broadcasters from all over Canada. The subject was one of my Dad's favourite themes, "Free Speech and Free Enterprise."

Keith Rogers was for free enterprise of course, but it was free enterprise that recognized its social responsibilities. He was convinced of the necessity for vocational training and adult education as there were none of these programs available on the Island at that time.

When Dr. John T. Croteau was teaching at St. Dunstan's University he, with other enthusiasts, organized Credit Unions and Co-operatives among the fishermen along the North Shore. The Credit Union was the first form of credit unrelated to the local merchant and from that, the Co-operatives developed. CFCY offered free, many hours of broadcast time to promote these forums where fishermen and farmers could talk about their problems. Keith Morrow helped to organize this series of programs. He also had one of the earliest regular agricultural programs. Before that talks would be given by experts on the subject but Keith did a noon market report for the farmers and added short features on agriculture. He was working at the Experimental Farm at the time and it was a tight squeeze to get into town on his lunch hour and do the broadcast. This was in the summer; in the winter he attended the Agricultural College in Guelph. One day the Superintendent of the Experimental Farm, who knew that Keith was doing these broadcasts, decided to keep him right up to the last moment and he arrived at the studio totally unprepared. He solved the problem by describing what he had done all morning. Having cleaned out the poultry shed, he told everyone about the virtues of hen manure and at one point used the more common expression for that product. He could hear peals of laughter from the office outside as studios in those days were not completely sound-proof. The staff were in stitches.

"Do you know what you said on the air?
You said hen shit three or four times!"

Either we had no listeners that day or hen shit is the accepted term on Prince Edward Island, whichever way it was, there were no complaints.

Our first regular agricultural commentator was Ches Cooper. He

157

wasn't hired to do this, it came about naturally. Ches, in fact, had great difficulty getting hired at the start. His first audition didn't go over very well with the Colonel who liked announcers to have deep-throated resonant voices. So Bob Large had to write Ches:

October 15, 1946

From R.F. Large, Program Manager

Dear Ches:

This morning I played your recording for the Colonel and he is of the opinion that there is little future for you in radio as an announcer. Kindest regards.

But Ches was determined and after the first letter he got in touch with the Colonel to ask for an appointment to talk it over. My Dad did change his mind and hired him which just goes to prove it doesn't pay to give up too easily. It was a shaky start to a career that lasted a lifetime and brought many rewards. Ches started out singing and announcing on his own show in the early morning and he remembers interviewing Wilf Carter and Johnny Cash and Hawkshaw Hawkins and sometimes Hank Snow. He recalled that "it was pretty early in the morning for

Courtesy of Canadian Broadcasting Corp

A. Keith Morrow.

these entertainers as they would be at Joey MacDonald's Sporting Club the night before and wouldn't get to bed until one o'clock but Wilf Carter would turn up in great good spirits at a quarter after seven in the morning. He'd be sitting there waiting for him. Ches couldn't get over this because Wilf Carter was a big star even at that time."

Ches originated "Checkerboard Chatter" the program that led him into agricultural broadcasting. "I didn't have the voice of course — Lorne Greene was our idol — but I just sort of developed my own style of broadcasting. I always had in mind that I wanted to be myself and not try to imitate anyone and I found that the audience reacted nicely to that". Ches explains his background this way: "I lived right in the village of Murray Harbor and my grandfather owned a farm at Gladstone and I spent a good amount of time there. I was exposed to fisheries and farming by living in a small village." That Checkerboard Chatter program led him eventually to the CBC in Halifax where he was host of "Country Calendar" and "Radio Noon".

Helen Herring as hostess on "To-day at Home", CFCY-TV 1960's.

On my desk are some early radio and television schedules of the 1940's and 50's and they bring back so many memories and remind me of interesting and varied programs. One of these was Helen Herring's, arranged by the Prince Edward Island Women's Institutes. Helen has been honoured at several national conventions of the Associated Country Women of the World for originating these weekly programs, the first Womens Institute radio programs on a weekly basis in Canada. This educational program began in 1948 and was on radio station CFCY for thirty-five consecutive years and during that time she interviewed hundreds of people. Her personality was warm and friendly and she was always well informed. She aired the concerns of women long before those concerns became nationally discussed.

The program had the support of the members, but other people listened as well, as Helen Herring suggested:

"The goals were to educate, really. From my letters I seem to recall that the people on the northern shore of Nova Scotia were avid listeners. Later I visited all of these places, Wallace, Tatamagouche, Pugwash and so on, and I was surprised and delighted that they welcomed me as a friend. They thought they knew me. I've always liked radio...you have to communicate your whole personality in your voice, and if you are able to do that, you are successful. You have to do your homework, and it is time consuming, but if you are talking to an author, it would be a courtesy at least to read the book that was being promoted."

In 1981 UPEI conferred on her an honorary Doctor of Laws Degree, and she called that "a humbling experience". One odd coincidence was the fact that when she came to town to go to Prince of Wales College at the age of fifteen, Helen Herring lived on Upper Hillsboro Street in 1924, at Walter Burke's home, and she told me that she used to play the piano downstairs some Sunday afternoons when my father and Walter Burke were working together, experimenting in radio. "They would be upstairs testing and they would call down to me to stop and then to start again:

"It was all, I imagine, pioneering and they were testing the apparatus. It was strange, I remember Colonel Rogers there and little did I think that I would ever be broadcasting myself for so many years. Radio in 1924 was hailed as just something wonderful. You were in sort of awe to think that there were all those sounds in the air, and by merely having this little machine, you

160

*got them, but they were there all the time. It did change com-
munity life. In Cape Traverse where I lived we learned about
places that we'd never heard of perhaps, or just read about.
Pittsburg was KDKA and WBZ in Springfield, Mass. They
became cities that we knew really well or thought we did."*

Some years stand out in memory more than others, and the year
1950 stands out as a sad one at CFCY. It was the year that Art McDonald
died at the early age of forty-seven. He had been seriously ill for five
years. It was Art who created the slogan, "Friendly Voice of the
Maritime" and it was Art who brought Don Messer to the station and
with Don created a program that meant so much to so many people
across Canada. He never forgot the sick and the shut-in listeners and
when he was on the air he would always play special selections for them.
He was buried in his birthplace in Souris, a place that he loved so well.

When Art died CFCY was in a period of upheaval. It was expanding
again. Dad had been advised that we would be able to use 5,000 watts
in the evening hours if he put in a new antenna system. Higher towers
would be needed and a wide area for a ground system. For weeks he
combed Queen's County for a suitable site, finally deciding on about
fifty acres at North River. It was a fortunate decision as later he found
out that the Trans-Canada Highway would go right past the front door
of the transmitter building.

Bob Large was Chief Engineer at that point, and the technical details
were left to him. It was a happy coincidence that he had as Technical
Supervisor Lorne Finley who carried the main work load, as Bob was
also Station Manager at the time.

It was the end of an era of the station building its own equipment.
My father was planning for the future and he decided to put the profits
of the company back into equipment. A new General Electric 5,000
watt transmitter was ordered and two towers just under three hundred
feet high were erected. George Morrison had gathered a crew once again
and was putting up a new transmitter building. Lorne Finley remembers
it as a "milestone". "We finally had an antenna that was directionally
controlled and we didn't have to go back to 1,000 watts at night". Bob
remembers it was mainly hard work. But finally as well as having a
spanking new transmitter, CFCY had a complete back-up transmitter
and a new diesel electric generator to give the listeners uninterrupted

service. Later, when CFCY was licenced to go to 10,000 watts, a third tower was added.

There was an apartment in the new transmitter building and Mona and Ray Simmons were resident transmitter operators. Ray picked up some technical knowledge and Mona learned to read the dials, turn on the diesel and do most of the ordinary duties but if she had real trouble on her shift she would call Doug Moser, Lorne Finley, John Phillips and later Walter Corney. A transmitter operator for twenty years, Mona loved to do the landscaping around the building and one year won the Provincial First Prize of the Rural Beautification Society for the beauty of the trees and shrubs she had planted.

While all these changes were being made to the radio station, my father's mind was on television. As far back as 1931 when he was forming a limited company, he had inserted in the Letters Patent, an unusual phrase. The Island Radio Broadcasting Co. Ltd. would be legally entitled, in carrying on the business of radio broadcasting,

"to send and transmit, receive and re-transmit by radio vision or otherwise, pictures."

Gord Johnston Photo

Receptionist and commercial writer, whose voice has also been heard on many commercials, Muriel Murtagh was honoured for 35 years of service in 1989.

He was thinking far ahead, twenty-five years or more, to the time when television would become a reality. One of the first television sets to arrive on Prince Edward Island was won in a Canada-wide contest for salesmanship in 1953 by Art Arsenault and my father eagerly knocked on his door and asked to see it. The television screen was in a large polished mahogany cabinet and there was a record-player and radio as well, a good thing as these were the only usable items. There was nothing on the screen except the usual "snow". Art was a musician and hoped one day to see some famous orchestras and artists. He had played the piano on CFCY in the early thirties when times were hard and it was sometimes so cold in the studio that Art would put on a tight-fitting pair of gloves when he played. I remember Art and his wife Claire playing duets and also when he played for Ken Cameron of Amherst who sang "Those Little White Lies". It was a song everyone requested. Art had studied under the legendary Professor S.N. Earle and with Father Theodore Gallant, a gifted organist. He tried his best to get something—anything—on that television screen. Dad would come every Sunday and they would try to find some faint image. For a long time there was nothing. Then suddenly one Sunday a hazy black and white picture leaped into life. It was a little man swinging back and forth on a trapeze. The three of them, Claire, Art and Dad huddled in excit- ment close to the screen as that little fellow swung back and forth. After that Dad ordered a television set from Chicago, although he would only get intermittent reception from distant stations at that time. Reception was best in the summer and my brother Bill remembers the first singer he saw and heard was Kate Smith, a picture received from Kansas City.

When Dad saw a demonstration of television at the World's Fair back in 1939 he realized that he would somehow have to raise a considerable amount of money if he wanted to build a television station in Prince Edward Island. All of the odds were against it. The population wasn't large enough to make it a viable enterprise. He sought the advice of friends in the industry and they told him "to invest the money and forget about television". As usual, this admonition only made him more determined.

I remember that he had an old atlas of Prince Edward Island that he had carefully marked to show the highest spots from which he would be able to send strong signals throughout the Island and into the neigh- bouring counties of Nova Scotia. One day we drove out to see the land

163

he had chosen at Strathgartney in the Bonshaw hills. My father was exuberant, proudly showing us every inch of the property. He had decided to put one of the original CFCY towers there indicating that television was coming. Pioneers of an earlier age would have said that he was "staking a claim".

He began making speeches to service clubs and organizations about television. He wasn't certain how he could finance the venture and he talked about the public sharing the cost. In his mind he was unwilling to risk the secure position of the radio station, but he was determined that somehow he would carry it through.

On January 12th, 1954, he addressed the Men's Association of Trinity United Church and told them that the tower had been placed in Bonshaw and assured them that "the chances of having television within the next few years are now very good."

One of the old original towers erected on top of hill at Bonshaw to show that television was coming.

For the past four years, my father had also been worrying about the family insurance business, W.K. Rogers Agencies. It was experiencing financial problems and it was an emotional as well as a financial drain. He would spend hours going over the books, coming back to CFCY in the late afternoons looking grey and tired and very old. He finally had to look for a purchaser and he found one. The "Colonel" suddenly looked years younger. His step was quick. He was back to his brim-full life.

Happiness can be very intense, and it can be very brief. Three days after celebrating his sixty-second birthday and just nine days after he had spoken to the Men's Association about television, my father died suddenly from a heart seizure.

His interest in communication had lasted a lifetime. He had been on the air using his amateur wireless transmitter VE1HI in the days just before he died, talking to Robert Griffiths at the isolated Hudson Bay Company store at Frobisher Bay on Baffin Island to relay the happy news that his wife had just given birth to a son at the Prince Edward Island Hospital. Mrs. Griffiths had talked to her husband in the North over my Dad's amateur wireless station.

I never heard my father say things like "I love life" or "I love people". He didn't need to. His humour, his sadnesses, his regrets, and his actions spoke these sentiments for him. Sometimes how a person feels about life and his fellow human beings can be reflected, caught, in the unasked-for gesture of another. For example, on the day of Dad's funeral, early morning snow had fallen, but when the family woke up it had all been removed from the driveway and the steps—from all up and down in front of the house. Charlie Chamberlain had come very early in the morning and shovelled all that snow. It was his way of showing his respect and love.

The funeral was a solemn military one and I can remember the young soldiers in their uniforms and the flowers. But mostly I remember the streets lined with people that Sunday afternoon. Many had been listeners to his Sacred Hour and other programmes he had started. From the church right out to the cemetery people stood quietly on the sidewalks or sat in their cars with their hats off as the funeral procession passed by.

Chapter Eighteen

Pictures
Out of
Thin Air

We were given very little time to mourn my father's death. All at once we were crowded in by lawyers, accountants and bank managers—experts. I'm afraid they only made more confusing the problems we had to face.

It was the opinion of these experts that now that Dad was gone, the affairs of CFCY would fall into chaos. They believed that Dad and Dad alone was responsible for all major decisions. However, what they didn't know was that it was Dad's style to instill two somewhat opposing qualities in almost everyone who worked for him: independence and complete reliability.

For example one of these gentlemen went through our accounting system with a fine tooth comb and condemned it as inefficient, outdated and cumbersome. We sat there amazed as he told us in awesome detail after detail how he would streamline our programming schedules and accounting. I could imagine us living in a veritable snowstorm of pink, yellow and green triplicate forms. What he didn't realize however was that Mickey Place, who could tally the Prince Edward Island election results and calculate the odds and scores at the Charlottetown Race track in his head, had a computer for a brain; and that Bob Large, with his perspicacity and profound common sense mixed with independence, saw immediately just how chaotic the experts' new-fangled systems would be. The independence and the reliability that had become so much a hallmark of working together made us say "NO!" to the experts. Bob put a stop to any thought of making major changes at a time when some

166

change was inevitable. Eventually the experts, seeing they could make no inroads, paraded sadly out. The air around us lightened, and we got on with our business.

After Dad's death, my mother was shattered. Grief consumed her to the point that she relied on her instincts in order to survive. She took Dad's death so terribly hard that for a while her memories became living realities in the present. Her Keith was always with her. Mother had become President of the company and for a time because of her grief it was difficult to make any decisions about the company's future. Whether or not we should go into television was one of the most difficult decisions facing us at this time.

A lifetime of bill paying, two heart attacks and constant worry to keep CFCY afloat had made my father somewhat reluctant to go through the whole process again with television. Yet the dream of television was as strong in him as his early dream of radio. He believed one way to bring television to Prince Edward Island—without the wear and tear he had suffered during his youth—was to go public, the people of the Island buying the shares. This idea was the subject of many speeches he had made throughout the Island shortly before his death.

Earlier, when Dad had been laid up with his heart attacks, Bob Large directed the day to day operations of the station. When he was just four-teen years old, Bob had had his own one-watt radio station, playing lively band concerts for family and neighbours. These were heard throughout a two or three-block radius of his father's home in Charlottetown. I remember that down through the years—years during which he played such an active, indispensable role in the life of CFCY—Bob always avoided the limelight. He was the one who, in a characteristic low-key and efficient manner, brought about the reality of CFCY Television.

Bob and my father had talked of television constantly—indeed, Dad had sent Bob on several research visits to television stations in upstate New York and in Bangor, Maine, these stations being comparable in size to a future Island station.

So, at the time of Dad's death, Bob had already accumulated five years of feasibility study. He now, without fuss, contacted his many asso-ciates in broadcasting, inquiring about the type of equipment needed and costs. A familiar phrase was thrown back at him: all his contacts advised "don't do it. Nothing good will come from it." But the decision had already been made.

Because of CFCY's outstanding relationship with such manufacturers as General Electric, Bob knew he could buy equipment on generous terms through a few select companies. Before the new station was ready to go on air, a year of intensive planning was required—not to mention a substantial increase in staff. We were confronted with a whopping investment of over a quarter of a million dollars—multiply that by ten and you will approximate today's equivalent. The pressures were enormous.

Bob gives a great deal of credit to his young assistant Lorne Finley at that time for taking a huge load off his shoulders. Lorne, who came from a small Island farming community, was one of those young men who seem to be born with a special knowledge. Armed only with a few correspondence courses on the technology of television transmission, Lorne—assisted by the installation staff of Canadian General Electric in Toronto—oversaw the technical installation at Strathgartney.

Strathgartney had been picked originally by Dad as the Island's highest suitable point for television transmission. The experts suggested that we should install a new and larger tower than the one Dad had installed earlier. The old tower which had been Dad's pride and joy held so much significance for us all. We couldn't believe that it was now considered short. It had been at West Royalty for so many years and with its twin was our first "high tower", transmitting programs over a wide area of the Maritimes. But technology often supersedes sentiment and a lofty and more modern one was ordered.

Upon reflection however, I'm sure if Dad had been alive he would have approved and enjoyed the building of this new tower. He had jubilantly scaled the old one, and I have no doubt he would have attempted to climb this new Everest which was 600 feet high, 936 feet above sea level, and which could direct power along the entire length of Prince Edward Island, and towards New Glasgow and Nova Scotia.

When we expanded from radio to television the old staff had to learn the new tricks of the new trade. Of course, working in a visual medium meant hiring people with visual skills, such as artists. Our first fulltime artist was young Henry Purdy, fresh from the Nova Scotia College of Art and Design and only just turned twenty.

As in the early days of radio, in the early days of television money was in short supply. Helen Herring, who had done so many womens' programs on radio, was about to be launched on her television program Today at Home. Bob called in the production crew and admonished young Henry: "No sets. We have no money for sets. Okay? No kitchen cupboards. Is that understood?"

The show went on. When it was over Bob rushed in to see Henry.

"I thought I told you there were to be no sets, no cupboards."

"But there weren't", replied Henry.

"But I saw them with my own eyes," Bob shot back.

"What you saw was a painting," said Henry. "I painted it all on a flat."

Incredulous, Bob ran back into the studio to check it out.

When Bob was figuring out the cost of the television station equipment, other broadcasters warned that we might risk everything we had, if the cost was too high, so he decided that there would be only one camera chain at the start. The afternoon I recall that one camera was behaving as it should with Barry MacLaren getting all the right shots of Helen Herring's interview. Then with no warning at all, it broke down completely. Henry Purdy happened to be right there and grabbing a Polaroid camera he started taking still pictures. The Polaroid developed the picture as Henry rushed upstairs to the control room, slapped the photo on a card and put it in a machine called a tellop. Then Henry would rush downstairs to take another shot. The interview went on as if nothing was happening. Viewers would see Mrs. Herring in a stark pose about to hand the guest some papers—the voice still coming over but no lips moving. The next shot would be of the guest learning forward. Then a side view of Mrs. Herring; it went on and on, like a giant step backward in time to the old stereopticon or magic lantern. Henry was young and agile and Mrs. Herring had a sense of humour. An amused audience scratched their heads in wonderment over what was happening to the modern medium of television.

My father had always considered that local interest, educational and public service programs were of the utmost importance. It was his firm belief that if a community broadcasting station was truly servicing its people, it was bound to have the character of the people it served. Dad had very strong convictions about how radio should not be used, and these could be summed up in the fact that broadcasting **should** be used in the interests of democracy and for the cultural reinforcement and development of its community. New ideas were always encouraged. One of these had come from Bob Large, who was Program Manager at that period in the 1940's when great changes were taking place in education

169

in the province. He had asked Helen MacDonald who was then provincial President of the Home and School Association, to begin a series of programs, "What's New in Home and School." Many aspects of the educational system were aired on this program in an innovative manner, and she was the resource person for "Challenge" initiated by Dr. David Boswell for teenagers, particularly students of the new high schools when they came into being. I remember once asking her to take on the added responsibility of looking after the participants of a new program on television for young people called "Teen Hop" for fifteen and sixteen year olds. Diane MacLellan (Blanchard) and "Mate" McIsaac were to be the young hosts with a young man of fourteen or fifteen who had an extensive record collection of note and would be spinning the platters. His name was Mike Duffy. He was a brash kid, full of energy and ambition, and he was determined to start his career right then and there, but no one would take him seriously. I imagine it was because of his age. Time of course proved that all of us were wrong. He is now one of Canada's most respected television journalists.

In grade 9 in school young Mike Duffy used to spin the records for "Teen Hop", CFCY TV, and wrote "Platter Chatter" for the Charlottetown Guardian.

During a span of thirty years, Helen's work evolved into "People Unlimited", a television program which she arranged and coordinated.

Helen confesses to always being nervous in front of a television camera. She could never get used to "the people jumping around behind the camera". All that action "off stage" terrified her. Perhaps her first experience on television had something to do with it.

The late Dr. Kenneth Parker was chairman of a panel early in the first year of CFCY television. None of the participants had ever been on television before, and panic and fright were common. The program was structured, and questions and answers were to be prepared in advance. Everything was "live" at the beginning and there was no way of videotaping a show. Material went on the air just as it was spoken. In some manner Dr. Parker gave out a set of questions to Helen MacDonald that were meant for Mrs. Basil McDonald from Tracadie and she got Helen's questions. The rehearsal was disoriented. Mrs. Basil McDonald, a devout member of the Roman Catholic church, became speechless; then out came: "Glory be to God", she said. "I'll never be able to do it." Beads of perspiration hung on her forehead. She was so shaken that Dr. Parker drew Helen aside: "Take her home for a cup of tea and calm her down!"

When they went back after supper, it was Mrs. Basil McDonald who sailed through with colors flying while Helen, faced with those two lights in front of the camera, shook like a jelly fish as the mixed-up questions came her way.

I am amazed at the echoes and parallels we found in television of radio. For example, radio had its famous disaster, the Moose River Gold Mine. Early television too had its disaster which electrified and coalesced the country—the Springhill Coal Mine disaster. The synthesis was completed. In addition to reading and hearing about it, people were seeing it.

Just as early listeners dressed up to listen to radio, early viewers of television had the feeling that as they were watching people on the screen, they in turn were being watched. Henry Purdy recalls, years later, a gentleman being surprised that Henry didn't recognize him.

"I don't see why not," the man said. "I watched you every blessed Friday night."

Perhaps the chilling things that George Orwell wrote about Big Brother came from this early effect television had on people. In any case, it points out again the power of the media—a power my father was ever aware of.

171

My father's radio station had gained momentum during a time when the world was polarizing. Nazi Germany was on the rise. In Spain it was Franco. My father was a small town businessman in Canada's smallest province; but he was more than this. He was a true patriot—not in the narrow redneck sense—but in the sense of his being a son of the Island and of Canada. He believed that the smaller parts had to be healthy in order to have a wholesome Canada.

One aspect of his ham radio set was his powerful short wave receiver. I remember the hateful, frenetic voice of Hitler and the frightening choruses of Seig Heil! Seig Heil! filling our home. Everything in that voice of hate was the direct opposite of my father's voice.

All his life he would lay stress on frèedom. Freedom of speech.. freedom to express creativity…freedom from the Hitlers of the world. As a boy, he had a dream, as a man he accomplished that dream although it was never easy. He truly believed that radio and later television could be harnessed for good. While "communicating with the world" he believed in freedom of expression; and that the voice of the people should always be heard loud and clear. I quote directly from a speech he gave to the Canadian Author's Association in 1942.

"Broadcasting, the press, and moving pictures… reach with equal power into the homes of the wealthy and most humble citizens…capable of immense force for good or evil…if free speech in radio is curtailed so likewise will freedom of speech or the written word be curtailed…The Hitlers, the Mussolinis and the Father Coughlins of every country are only too eager and anxious to capture the imagination of the world…radio has the means to perpetuate their power, or if used wisely it can create the vision of a world of beauty and peace; a world where spiritual values can take their rightful place; a world in which little children can again laugh and sing, a world where their parents may rest with reasonable security in the hope they will not wake up some morning to find it shattered in rubble around them."

CFCY Radio and CFCY-TV Staff

1922 - 1971

They were talented, productive and creative. May their prototypes spring up everywhere in radio and television stations across Canada.

Adams, John Quincy
Alexander, John R.
Balcolm, Mac
Balderson, Marlene
Beagan, Doreen
Beer, Joyce (Nicholson)
Beers, George
Birch, Carol
Birt, Gerry
Blair, Phyllis (Hooper)
Bonnell, Catherine
Bourgeau, Wanda (MacMillan)
Brehaut, John
Brown, Arlene (MacDonald)
Brown, William J.
Buchanan, Mary
Buel, Alton
Cameron, Jack
Campbell, Ann (Duffy)
Campbell, Colin
Campbell, Elizabeth
Carrier, Judy
Carter, Wilfred Brenton (Whit)
Clarke, Helen (White)
Clark, Connie (MacLeod)
Cochrane, Gordon D. (Tex)
Cochrane, Ian, D.

Cole, Beth (McLaine)
Compton, Charles
Connolly, Felix
Cook, Carolyn
Cooper, Ches
Cooper, Colin
Corkum, Max
Corney, Walter
Cox, Betty (Doyle)
Craswell, Coris
Cross, Jim
Crozier, Marilyn (Boswell)
Daley, Hartwell
Dalziel, Marjorie (Hooper)
Dickson, Havelock, H.
Dickson, A. Stuart
Dinsdale, Frances (MacMillan)
Duncan, Joe
Easter, Frank
Fanjoy, John
Ferguson, Douglas
Fielding, John
Finley, A. Lorne
Fisher, Ed.
Fitzgerald, Flora (Wiggins) Flo
Fitzgerald, William
Flemming, Richard

Ford, Kathy (Buchanan)
Fraser, Arthur
Fraser, F. Murray
Fraser, George
Frizzell, Marjorie
Gallant, Vince
Gamble, Blair
Gibson, Dave
Gish, Adele (Coyle)
Gordon, Janet
Graham, Bill
Hale, Ted
Hannon, Mary (McInnis)
Hart, George
Hellmich, Christina
Hennessey, Harold
Henry, Bob
Holman, Reginald
Hoyt, Alexander, (Sandy)
Hunt, William S.
Hunter, Ian
Jackson, Joyce
Jay, John
Johnston, Gord
King, Art
Large, Alex
Large, Betty (Rogers)
Large, Brenda M.
Large, Robert F. (Bob)
Leith, A.
LeLacheur, Clayton
Lewis, Frank
MacArthur, Charles
MacArthur, Wayne
MacCannell, Wendell
MacDonald, Borden
MacDonald, David
MacEwen, Eric
MacEwen, John

MacDonald, Kent
MacDonald, L.A. (Art)
MacEwen, Nora (Downe)
MacFarlane, Fred
MacFarlane, Vern
MacFarlane, Victor
MacKinnon, Allison
MacLaren, Barry
MacLennan, Edward
MacLeod, Bob
MacLeod, Jacqueline (Jackie)
MacLeod, Marjorie
MacMaster, Angus
MacMillan, George (Pud)
MacNeill, Hilton, J.
MacNevin, David
MacNutt, James
MacPhail, Vivian
MacPhee, Muriel (Campbell)
MacPherson, Harvey
MacPherson, Scott
McAdam, Ethel (Kelly)
McAulay, Loman
McCormack, Jerry
McDonald, Lewis
McQuaid, F.J.
Meyers, Elliot
Miles, Dick
Mitchell, Eleanor Mary (Duffy)
Morrison, George
Morrison, Gordon
Morrison, Lloyd
Morris, Jack
Morrow, Andrew
Morrow, Keith
Morrow, Marianne (Rogers)
Moser, Doug
Murley, Elaine
Murley, J. (Buller)

Murphy, Beverly (Hatton)
Murphy, Leon
Murtagh, Muriel (Sinnott)
Newman, Stan
Nichsolson, Jean
Palmer, Ingram
Partridge, Shirley (Lewis)
Peppin, Les
Perry, Lorne
Phillips, John
Place, J.T. (Mickey)
Pugh, Coralee
Pulsifer, Orville
Purdy, Henry
Putnam, Arthur G.
Rogers, Keith Sinclair
Rogers, William K.
Rogerson, Maida
Rose, Lloyd
Sampel, Hal
Scales, Doris (Hillion)
Scales, Joan
Schwartz, Dale
Schyler, Gretchen (Walters)
Secondcost, Ev.
Sentner, Adeline
Sentner, Carl
Semple, Beryl
Shaw, Donna
Shaw, Kathryn (Large)
Shelfoon, A.F. (Tony)
.Simmons, Bob
Simmons, Mona
Simmons, Ray
Simpson, Jim
Smith, Fred (Smitty)
Stetson, Gordon
Stewart, Ira
Stewart, John

Sullivan, Vaughn
Sutherland, Elmer
Swan, Blair
Tait, Gordon
Tait, Janet (Spillett)
Taylor, Brent
Taylor, Lynn
Thompson, Ken
Tupper, Alfred
Turgeon, Frank
Vail, Percy
Vaughn, Guy
Wade, Jim
Wakelin, Margaret
Walters, Esther, (MacDougall)
Watters, Ed.
White, Norma
Wigmore, Bob
Williams, Paul
Wood, Barbara (Cudmore)
Wood, Doug
Wooten, Joe
Young, Jeff
Young, Merrill, M.F.

Bibliography

Aird Commission, speech by Keith Rogers, Oct. 13, 1952, Y's Men's Club.

Allard, T.J., 1979, "Straight Up", Private Broadcasting in Canada 1918-1958; The Canadian Communications Foundation.

Barrett, John I., 1986, "Who's Who on Prince Edward Island."

Bird, Michael J., "The Town That Died", a chronicle of the Halifax Explosion; McGraw-Hill Ryerson Ltd. 1962.

"Broadcasting Stations in Canada"; The Canadian Association of Broadcasters.

Coyle, James J., Anniversary Issue, *"The Jimmy Journal"*. Hornby, James, *Island Magazine,* 1979," The Great Fiddling Contests of 1926".

Interviews taped by Tom Crothers, Betty Large and Dorothy MacDonald, 1986 and 1987.

MacDonald, Helen, Collection of interviews, Public Archives of Prince Edward Island.

Nowlan, Alden, *Week-End Magazine,* March 24, 1979, "Don Messer's Jubilee".

Sellick, Lester B., "Canada's Don Messer", 1969.

Settel, Irving, "A Pictorial History of Radio"; Grosset and Dunlap, 1967.

Stewart, Sandy, 1975 "A Pictorial History of Radio in Canada"; Toronto, Gage, 1957.

Index

Betty Rogers Large is a retired broadcaster. She and her husband, Bob Large live in Charlottetown. They have three daughters, Brenda, Editorial writer with the Whig-Standard, Kingston, Ontario; Daphne Scott an Island potter and Kathryn Shaw, CBC Journalist.

Tom Crothers has been an English teacher for twenty-five years. He has had a long asociation with theatre, particularly in the area of directing, writing and teaching. Tom lives with his wife the former Bessie Rodd from Harrington, Prince Edward Island, in Ontario.